table of
contents

The DEAD SEA Scrolls

Biblical Archaeology Society
Society of Biblical Literature
Washington, DC • Atlanta

introduction

This book was inspired by a fascinating exhibit supported by the Israel Antiquities Authority and the Dead Sea Scrolls Foundation and appearing at museums throughout the United States. In fact, the book was designed to supplement the exhibit, providing visitors and other interested readers with a full historical and photographic account of the Dead Sea Scrolls, from their initial discovery in 1947 to their recent publication and ongoing interpretation. Within this volume readers will learn not only how the Dead Sea Scrolls were found but also why many scholars believe that other scrolls still await discovery. In addition to becoming acquainted with both the Scrolls themselves and the ancient group who originally wrote them, readers will find out why the Dead Sea Scrolls continue to be significant for the Jewish and Christian religions today.

Each of the chapters that follow, which first appeared in *Biblical Archaeology Review* or *Bible Review,* has been written by a recognized expert on the Dead Sea Scrolls.

* **Harry Thomas Frank** draws on his experience as an archaeologist and historian to recount the exciting tale of the Scrolls' discovery and acquisition.

* **Baruch Safrai,** who continues to excavate in the region, supplements Frank's account by presenting evidence that additional scrolls and archaeological "treasures" remain undiscovered within the barren Judean Desert.

* **Frank Moore Cross,** Harvard University professor and Dead Sea Scrolls' translator, introduces readers to the Scrolls and their likely authors, the ancient Essenes.

* **Emanuel Tov,** editor-in-chief of the official publication series of the Scrolls, describes the obstacles that he and other scholars faced and overcame to ensure the full publication of the Scrolls.

* **Sidnie White Crawford** melds her expertise as a Scrolls editor and textual critic to show what the Dead Sea Scrolls teach us about the fluidity of the biblical text during the early years of the Common Era (C.E.).

* **James C. VanderKam,** University of Notre Dame professor and likewise a Scrolls editor, identifies how the Qumran community and early Christianity were similar in some ways yet each unique.

* **Lawrence H. Schiffman,** author of numerous volumes on the Scrolls and ancient Judaism, offers a new perspective on what the Scrolls teach us about the varieties of Judaism of the last century B.C.E. and the first century C.E.

We trust that readers will find this pictorial and narrative journey to the ancient ruins of Qumran and through the Dead Sea Scrolls informative, invigorating, and enlightening as they gain not only insight into the long-forgotten history of the Qumran community but also understanding of the ongoing significance of the Scrolls for people today.

A ROMAN WILDERNESS ROUTE TURNED PATH OF DISCOVERY

GENERAL VIEW, LIMESTONE CLIFFS AT QUMRAN

Before the discovery of the Scrolls, most archaeologists assumed the ruins of Qumran were the remains of one of the many small forts the Romans erected throughout the wilderness to control the natural travel routes along the western shore of the Dead Sea between Jericho and Masada. A formal excavation of the site was conducted from 1951 to 1956 by the Jordanian Department of Antiquities.

The white building surrounded by trees is the visitors center, which was built after excavations were completed. At the right is the floor of Wadi Qumran, which over the centuries sculpted the southern face of the marl terrace.

HOW THE DEAD SEA SCROLLS WERE FOUND

By Harry Thomas Frank

The most sensational archaeological discovery of the last half century was made entirely by accident. On a morning in the winter of 1946–1947 three shepherds of the Ta'amireh tribe of Bedouin watched their nimble-footed goats skip across the cliffs just north of an old ruin on the northwest shore of the Dead Sea. The ruin, known as the City of Salt, is mentioned in the Old Testament (Joshua 15:62), and from time to time archaeologists had shown interest. But from the middle of the nineteenth century, when they first worked in the area, until those days in winter, they had said that there was not much at that desolate site. Possibly it was a minor Roman fort. Perhaps, some of the more fanciful suggested, it was even Gomorrah!

About a mile to the south of the ruin is one of the larger of the numerous freshwater springs that surround the Dead Sea. This place, known as 'Ain Feshkha, is where these three Bedouin watered their animals. Then it was up the cliffs and into the forbidding wilderness where shepherds, like David of the ancient past, let their flocks wander in search of food. And so on that fateful day the immemorial scene was repeated, with black beasts defying gravity on steep inclines, leaping, stopping to nibble here and there.

A seemingly disinterested shepherd moved leisurely below, but his eye missed nothing. Some of the goats were climbing too high up. It was getting late and time to get them down. Jum'a Muhammed—that was the name of the fellow—now showed his own nimbleness in getting up the cliff face. As he climbed, something caught his attention. There were two small openings in the rock. They were caves, or maybe two openings into the same cave. But they were so small. A man could not get through the lower one but might just squeeze through the upper one.

He threw a rock into the opening and then peered in. He had clearly heard the rock break pottery—what else would be in these remote caves but long-hidden treasure? Maybe his days of following the sheep were soon to be over. He peered ever more intently into the black depths of the cave, but nothing could be made out. Excitedly, he yelled down to his two cousins, calling them to join him on the cliff face. Khalil Musa

Cousins, Caves, and Timeless Treasures

As the story is told, a Bedouin shepherd boy tossed a stone into a cave (at left) hoping to find a stray goat from his flock. But instead of a bleat, he heard the sound of breaking pottery.

Jum'a Muhammed (left) and Muhammed edh-Dhib (Muhammed the Wolf) are the two Ta'amireh Bedouin cousins who claim they discovered the first Dead Sea Scrolls in 1947. Accounts differ as to which cousin first noticed the cave, but Muhammed the Wolf is credited as the first to enter the cave and find the first scrolls. That morning the cousins carried three scrolls back to their camp. Those scrolls were probably the complete Isaiah Scroll, the Manual of Discipline, and the Habakkuk Commentary. The cousins discovered four more intact scrolls from the cave in the following weeks. Over the next decade, members of the same Bedouin clan discovered four more caves that held scroll remains.

was older. Muhammed Ahmed el-Hamed was younger, a teenager. They came up and heard the fantastic tale. But it was now getting very late, and the goats had to be gathered. Tomorrow would take them to 'Ain Feshkha. In the afternoon they would return for another look at this intriguing cave.

They did not visit the cave the next afternoon, returning somewhat later than planned from 'Ain Feshkha. At dawn of the next morning Muhammed Ahmed el-Hamed, who was nicknamed "The Wolf" (edh-Dhib), woke first. Leaving his two cousins sleeping on the ground, he scaled the 350 or so feet up to the cave Jum'a had found two days before.

With effort the slender young man was able to lower himself feet first into the cave. The floor was covered with debris, including broken pottery. But along the wall stood a number of narrow jars, some with their bowl-shaped covers still in place. Edh-Dhib scrambled over the floor of the cave and plunged his hand into one of the jars. Nothing. Frantically, he tore the cover from another, eagerly exploring the smooth inside of the empty container. Another and yet another with the same result. The ninth was full of dirt.

The increasingly desperate young Bedouin at last closed his hand around something wrapped in cloth. He extracted two such bundles and then a third, which had a leather covering but not a cloth wrapping. The cloth and the leather were greenish with age. These were all that edh-Dhib took from the cave that morning.

He wiggled himself out of the opening and half-ran, half-fell down the hillside to show his sleepy cousins what he had found. Treasure indeed! Scholars who later interviewed edh-Dhib think that this boy had in his hands on that winter morning nothing less than the great Isaiah Scroll, the Habakkuk Commentary, and the Manual of Discipline!

Khalil and Jum'a could not have been less interested in the ancient scrolls that edh-Dhib showed them.

Where was the treasure? Had he hidden it for himself? Eventually edh-Dhib was able to convince the other two that he had found nothing but these "worthless" rolls. Had he looked carefully? Maybe there were other jars. Maybe one of the broken ones had spilled its valuable contents onto the floor of the cave and it was in the debris.

Once more the three made their way up the hill to the cave. Edh-Dhib passed a number of jars out of the opening, but these were left in front of the cave when they proved to be empty, just as he had said. Downcast, the shepherds zigzagged their way down to the makeshift camp. Jum'a crammed the rolls into a bag. When later they returned to the Ta'amireh center near Bethlehem, he took them with him. The bag with its "treasure" was hung on a tentpole. How long it was there we do not know. Occasionally its contents were removed and passed around among more curious members of the tribe. The Isaiah Scroll was damaged, but only its cover. The precious text was unhurt. When the Manual of Discipline reached St. Mark's Monastery in Jerusalem some months later, it was in two pieces. But no one is sure if this was the fault of the Ta'amireh. The break is such that it could have occurred in ancient times.

A few weeks after the initial discovery of this cave—which came to be known to scholars as Qumran Cave 1, the cave of the great scrolls—Jum'a returned with other Bedouin and removed several other scrolls that they found there. As nearly as it is possible to reconstruct the story now, they removed seven major manuscripts altogether, the four that ended up at St. Mark's and the three that came into the possession of Hebrew University.

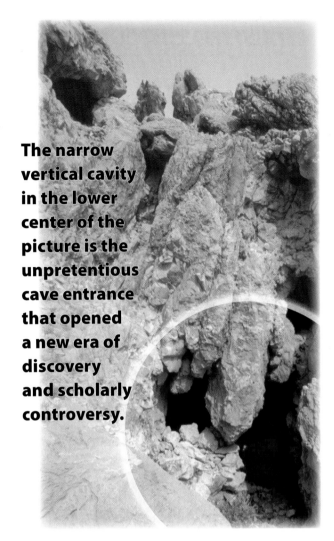

The narrow vertical cavity in the lower center of the picture is the unpretentious cave entrance that opened a new era of discovery and scholarly controversy.

Such was the discovery of the Dead Sea Scrolls, manuscripts a thousand years older than the then oldest known Hebrew texts of the Bible, manuscripts many of which were written a hundred years before the birth of Jesus and at least one of which may have been written almost three hundred years before the journey of Mary and Joseph to Bethlehem.

How these manuscripts got from a Bedouin tentpole into the scholar's study is as fascinating as their chance discovery. The setting for this part of the story

Safe Storage for the Scrolls

The scrolls found in Cave 1 had been carefully preserved in pottery vessels like the one shown here. The unusual shape suggests that they might have been made specifically for storing scrolls. Other examples of this type of jar were recovered from more than two dozen other caves in the vicinity. Later excavations of the ruins at Khirbet Qumran yielded the same type of pottery and a potter's kiln. These vessels are evidence linking the scrolls to the community at Qumran.

KANDO THE COBBLER

In Bethlehem, four of the seven scrolls from Cave 1 ended up in the hands of this man, Khalil Iskander Shahin (known as "Kando"), shown here in his shop. Kando was a Syrian Christian and a cobbler who also dealt in antiquities.

Kando appears to have been interested in the scrolls only for their monetary value, not for their potential as important historical artifacts.

was the last days of the British Mandate in Palestine. His Majesty's Foreign Office had somewhat irresponsibly decided that, since the problem of Palestine could not be solved by reason, they would withdraw, leaving the two sides to decide the issue by blood. Jewish and Arab families who had lived side by side for generations were being wrenched apart by fear and distrust. Barbed wire appeared in the most unlikely places. Immigrants, legal and illegal, added impetus to the worsening situation. Murders were growing in number. The King David Hotel in Jerusalem was blown up, with severe loss of life. In such times the Bedouin youths wondered if they could find a buyer for their greenish rolls.

n early April 1947 Jum'a and Khalil took the scrolls to Bethlehem, principal market town of the Ta'amireh. They took three scrolls and two jars to the carpenter shop of Ibrahim 'Ijha, who dabbled in antiquities. Faidi Salahi, another dealer in antiquities, was there. He was later to play a large role in the story of the scrolls, but on this occasion he cautioned 'Ijha to be careful. These things might be stolen. There might be serious trouble. The two shepherds moved on, carrying their jars and their scrolls.

In the marketplace, Jum'a, with the scrolls, ran into George Ishaya Shamoun, who was often in Bethlehem on Saturdays selling cloaks to Bedouin. Jum'a imparted

WHAT PRICE FOR HISTORY?

Kando gave the Bedouin the equivalent of approximately $20 on account, with the understanding that he and the man who had directed them to him would receive one-third of whatever he could get for the scrolls. He then set out to find a private buyer. It was seven years before the scrolls reached a scholar's hands and were given professional care.

Kando later was involved in the sale of the vast cache excavated by the Bedouin in Cave 4 and in prolonged negotiations over the last Dead Sea Scroll, the Temple Scroll from Cave 11.

the tale of these worthless scrolls to his friend. Someone suggested that they go to the cobbler's shop of Khalil Iskander Shahin—better known as Kando. Kando was a Syrian Orthodox Christian. He was also serious about the scrolls. For one-third of whatever the sale price might be, Kando and George would handle the disposal of the scrolls. Agreed. Jum'a and Khalil were given £5, and the scrolls were left in the little shop in Bethlehem.

During Holy Week, George, also Syrian Orthodox, mentioned the manuscripts to Athanasius Yeshue Samuel, Syrian Orthodox Metropolitan of Jerusalem. He told the priest that they were written in Syriac, wrapped "like mummies," and were from the wilderness near the Dead Sea. Samuel knew that they would have to be very old, if genuine, because that region had not been inhabited since early Christian times. He expressed an interest in the scrolls and urged Kando to bring them to St. Mark's.

Within the week Kando and George were at the monastery with one manuscript, the Manual of Discipline. It was, the Metropolitan saw at once, written not in Syriac but in Hebrew. Then, to the astonishment of his visitors, he broke off a piece of the margin and burned it. By this somewhat crude but effective means he determined it was animal skin. Yes, Samuel would buy this scroll and any others the Bedouin might have. Kando, manuscript securely in hand, departed but promised to get in touch with his friends from the desert. For several days anxious calls went out from St. Mark's to Kando's shop. The conversations were fruitless. Weeks went by. Samuel's frustration turned to resignation.

On the first Saturday in July, Kando called. Two Bedouin had brought some scrolls to Bethlehem. "Would they risk bringing them to Jerusalem?" asked Samuel. Yes. The tide of violence between Jew, Arab, and Briton was swelling. The worst was yet to come, but it was already a difficult and dangerous time in and around Jerusalem. In this atmosphere Samuel became anxious when the Bedouin had not appeared by noon. Yet he had not mentioned his appointment to anyone, since he was not entirely sure that the whole affair was not some kind of hoax. Hungry, agitated, Samuel

sat down to eat. In the idle lunchtime conversation Samuel heard one father mention that he had turned away some Bedouin from the door earlier that morning. When questioned, he affirmed that they had been carrying scrolls. The Syrian monk had even ascertained that they were written in Hebrew—probably old Torahs from somewhere, but filthy and covered with pitch or something smelling equally as bad. These he had steadfastly refused to allow within the monastery walls, still less into His Grace's presence, as they had demanded.

> **The scroll initially called by scholars the Manual of Discipline was probably known to those who first read it as the Rule of the Community. It contains rules and regulations for a devout separatist Jewish group.**

Samuel returned to his office to call Kando. As he reached for the telephone, it rang. It was none other than the Bethlehem parishioner himself, gravely offended at the treatment given his friends. Explanations were offered and apologies made. Where were the scrolls now? Thanks entirely to George, said Kando, they were safely back in Bethlehem.

It seems that when the Bedouin, along with George, who was the man closest to the shepherds in all this, had been turned away from the monastery, they went to the Jaffa Gate to catch the bus back to Bethlehem. There, in discussion with a Jewish merchant, an offer was made to buy the scrolls. George, however, had correctly guessed what the trouble had been at the door of St. Mark's. He was, furthermore, committed to the Metropolitan. He argued with his friends and

Like most of the other scrolls discovered at Qumran, the Isaiah Scroll was written on animal-skin panels sewn together with linen thread.

The Ageless Isaiah Scrolls

The best-preserved scroll from Cave 1 is the complete scroll of the book of Isaiah, all 66 chapters. This is also the longest document (23.5 feet) from any of the caves, with the exception of the last scroll, the so-called Temple Scroll, which was discovered in 1956. This was one of two scrolls of Isaiah found in Cave 1. Eventually, fragments from at least twenty other copies of this book were found in the Dead Sea caves. Isaiah was clearly one of the most revered writings in the Qumran library

One of the remarkable characteristics of this scroll is that, although it was written as early as 125 to 100 B.C.E., the text differs very little from the Masoretic Hebrew text (the "received text" in Jewish tradition) as it was previously known from manuscripts written one thousand years later.

finally prevailed. The three men, with manuscripts securely in hand, boarded the bus back to Bethlehem. Kando reached for his telephone when he heard what had happened. The incident at the Jaffa Gate, it should be noted, is not well authenticated and may be a part of the considerable legend that has grown up around the Dead Sea Scrolls.

It was another two weeks before Kando could make his way to Jerusalem. He was graciously received by the Syrian fathers. Samuel heard the story of the discovery of the cave and its contents. Of greater interest, five scrolls, including the one that had been brought previously, were produced from a bag. Two documents were in a delicate state. Two others looked similar and later proved to be the two halves of the Manual of Discipline. The fifth, the largest, was superbly preserved. It could be easily unrolled, revealing graceful Hebrew characters. A deal was made on the spot. The Metropolitan gave Kando £24 (roughly $97.00), of which two-thirds went to Jum'a and Khalil.

Three months after Samuel had first heard of the existence of the scrolls, they were in his possession. Now doubts began to creep in. Were they genuine? Was there such a cave as had been described to him? With George's help, Father Yusef, one of the monks from St. Mark's, visited the site and reported to his superior that there was such a cave and that it indeed contained scraps of other scrolls as well as a large jar suitable for storing much water.

With his faith in the authenticity of the scrolls revived, the Metropolitan set out to determine their contents and to sustain or destroy his view that they were from early Christian times. One would think that in a city such as Jerusalem, with its multiplicity of religious communities and prestigious scholarly institutions, this would have been a relatively simple matter. But few things are simple in Jerusalem, still less in a time of violence and when the question at hand is so patently improbable as authenticating scrolls two thousand years old. It was six months before Samuel's dreams were confirmed.

His first contact was the Palestine Department of Antiquities in the person of Stephen Hanna Stephen, a member of the Syrian Orthodox Church and thus well known to Samuel. There had been reports in Byzantine and earlier times of scrolls having been found near Jericho (Qumran is seven and a half miles south). From the second, third, and fourth Christian centuries came reports of Greek and Hebrew books found in jars in the area. Origen, an early church father, is said to have used some of these in compiling his famous Hexapla. In the late eighth century Patriarch Timothy I reported a similar find, noting that the manuscripts were found in caves. These things, common knowledge among scholars, were apparently not known to Stephen. But he did know of numerous incidents of hoaxes involving antiquities. He responded to the Metropolitan by suggesting the embarrassment that might come should his manuscripts turn out to be fake. Would Stephen, asked Samuel, call the documents to the attention of those in the Department of Antiquities who might be able to render proper judgment? Stephen preferred not to, lest he, too, be held up to ridicule before his colleagues.

The Syrian priest, undaunted by this rebuke, now found his way to the famous École Biblique, the Dominican monastery of St. Stephen and home of the French Biblical and Archaeological School. There he was received by Father Marmardji, a fellow Syrian and friend of long-standing, who listened to the story of the finding of the scrolls with interest. Some days later Father Marmardji came to St. Mark's accompanied by a young Dutch Dominican, Father J. Van der Ploeg. Together they examined the materials. Neither thought the writings were as old as claimed. The Dutchman did, however, immediately recognize the largest scroll as the book of Isaiah. He was the first to do so. When he returned to the École, Van der Ploeg spoke with some enthusiasm of the documents he had just seen. L. H. Vincent, a distinguished Dominican scholar and a fixture at the French monastery for

REVERED WRITINGS, REQUIRED READINGS

The Manual of Discipline was one of several sectarian documents, writings clearly produced by a particular group of a religious sect for use by the members, found among the Dead Sea Scrolls. Eventually, fragments of about ten copies of the Manual of Discipline were retrieved from Cave 4 and fragments of at least one more from Cave 5. This document was apparently "required reading" for members of some group in the area.

This manual was important to scholars because it strengthened the argument that the scrolls were placed in the caves by members of an organized religious settlement and identified some of the distinctive practices of that group. A number of scholars were quick to suggest that the group for whom the Manual of Discipline was written might have been the "Essenes," whom Josephus described as highly religious, apocalyptic in their beliefs, communal and ascetic in their practices, and, for the most part, celibate.

forty years, noted that this was the Dutch monk's first visit to Jerusalem and suggested that he should not be taken in so easily. If Samuel could produce pottery from the alleged context where the writings had been found, it might help to sustain his claims. When no pottery was forthcoming, Van der Ploeg did not pursue the matter further.

Samuel continued to seek scholarly help with the scrolls and even attempted to learn Hebrew. At one point a chance business contact resulted in the inspection of the scrolls by two men from the library of Hebrew University. They said they wished to photograph a few parts for further study. The monastery was placed at their disposal for such purposes, but they never returned, perhaps because of the increasing danger to a Jew in the Old City. A little later an antiquities dealer suggested sending the manuscripts to Europe or America, where they could be evaluated. But with postal services breaking down under the weight of civil conflict, Samuel thought it a bad idea to place his materials in the mails.

GATHERING THE PIECES TO A PRECIOUS PUZZLE

Scroll fragments — brought in a cardboard box, jumbled together as they had been found — are being separated and sorted, prior to being placed between sheets of glass. The job proved to be almost overwhelming for the small team and consumed much of their time in the ensuing years. Their initial funding grant ran out in 1960.

Yigael Yadin (on the right) is seen here with James Biberkraut, a Jewish refugee from Germany who expertly assisted Professor Sukenik in carefully unrolling the first Dead Sea Scrolls. Yadin was instrumental in acquiring the remaining scrolls from Cave 1 and, eventually, the Temple Scroll from Cave 11.

In late January 1948 the St. Mark's manuscripts came temporarily into the hands of E. L. Sukenik, the distinguished archaeologist of Hebrew University. Unknown to all but a very few, Sukenik had had other scrolls from the Bedouin's discovery in his hands since the previous November. Anton Kiraz now enters the story. Kiraz was a parishioner at St. Mark's and extremely close to Samuel. Sukenik had excavated on some of Kiraz's property in 1945 and was also personally known to him. Kiraz was thus admirably situated to act as contact between the priest and the professor.

Kiraz arranged for Sukenik to see the scrolls at the YMCA, which was in neutral territory at that time. As soon as he saw them, Sukenik made an offer of £100 for the materials, as Kiraz recalled. Sukenik, in his written recollection of the event, did not mention an offer. Whatever the facts, Kiraz allowed one scroll to be removed to Hebrew University for further study. The other documents remained in a drawer at the YMCA. The Isaiah Scroll stayed at the university for about a week, during which time some of it was hastily and somewhat incorrectly copied. When it was returned, Sukenik spoke of the university's interest in purchasing all of the scrolls.

According to Kiraz, the professor mentioned a purchase price of £500 ($2,025). Kiraz said he had to talk with Samuel. Sukenik is said to have increased the offer to £1,000 (£750 for Kiraz, £250 for Samuel), but Kiraz insisted on talking with the Metropolitan. He would contact Sukenik once he had had a chance to discuss the offer. At this juncture, in early February and fully a year after edh-Dhib had first slithered into the cave, Samuel's lifelong friend and fellow monk Butros Sowmy returned to St. Mark's. He was a learned man of good judgment. With increasing concern he heard of Sukenik's offer and of Samuel's apparent readiness to accept it. If Sukenik were so anxious to secure these documents, he reasoned, perhaps it would be wise to get another opinion. Kiraz wrote to the distraught professor saying they were not going to sell just now but would wait until the local situation settled a bit and they could perhaps get some international judgments or overseas offers.

In the meantime, Sowmy recalled his cordial dealings with the American Schools of Oriental Research just north of the Old City, near the École Biblique.

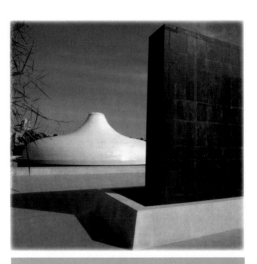

AN HONORABLE HOMECOMING

More than seven years after they were removed from Cave 1, the four scrolls finally returned to Jerusalem and were reunited with the other three scrolls from Cave 1. All seven of the Cave 1 scrolls were eventually installed in the Shrine of the Book, a building specially constructed to house them on the grounds of the Israel Museum in Jerusalem.

The scrolls are displayed beneath this gleaming dome, shaped to suggest the lid of a Dead Sea Scroll jar. The structure includes an underground "safe room" with steel walls, nearly 1.5 feet thick, a bomb shelter for the scrolls in case of enemy attack. (The scrolls were moved to the shelter during the Scud missile attacks on Israel in the 1991 Persian Gulf War.)

He telephoned, and the call was turned over to John Trever, a fellow of the school who had been left in temporary charge during the absence of Millar Burrows, the director. Sowmy asked if Trever would help date some old manuscripts that had been lying about St. Mark's library for some years. As a precaution, the Americans had not gone into the Old City for some time. It was now dangerous in the extreme. Could the materials be brought to the school? Sowmy agreed to present himself and the scrolls the next day at 2:30 P.M.

When they met again the following afternoon, Trever examined the manuscripts with mounting excitement. The writing on the Isaiah Scroll, although clearly Hebrew, was strange. Still, he had seen a similar script somewhere. On Trever's desk was a series of slides dealing with the background of the English Bible. He extracted a picture of the ninth-century C.E. British Museum Codex. The writing on the scrolls brought by Sowmy was older.

Trever then removed a slide of the Nash Papyrus, a second-century fragment: the Hebrew script was similar but not exactly the same. It was hard to be sure; the slide was much too small for detailed comparison in the hand viewer. After copying by hand that portion of the manuscript open before him, Trever proposed to Sowmy that a complete photographic record be made of all the scrolls. The monk was agreeable but said he would have to discuss it with his superior.

Beneath the dome of the Shrine of the Book, the scrolls belonging to the State of Israel are displayed in an environment where both climate and lighting are strictly controlled. The central position is occupied by the 23.5-foot-long complete Isaiah Scroll, which is mounted so that visitors can walk completely around it. The top of the display housing is in the shape of a Torah-scroll holder.

The rest of the day Trever and William Brownlee culled from the American Schools library all the material they could find about ancient manuscripts. Unfortunately, fighting interrupted Jerusalem's electric service that afternoon. But after working by kerosene lamps late into the night, the two men were convinced that the form of the script on the Isaiah Scroll was as old as or older than the Nash Papyrus.

The next day dawned bright—on the outside. The lights were still out inside the school. By 9:30 the Metropolitan and Father Sowmy were there with the materials to be photographed. Just as Trever was about to use natural light from a window, the electric lights came on. With Brownlee's assistance, the Isaiah Scroll and the Habakkuk Commentary were unrolled and photographed. By late afternoon the task was not complete. Three scrolls remained. But by this time the two Americans had won the confidence of the Syrian, who gladly left the unrecorded scrolls and a fragment behind as he returned to St. Mark's. Among the many happenstances surrounding the scrolls, none was more felicitous than the presence of so fine a photographer as Trever. His record of the contents of the four Dead Sea Scrolls from the Syrian monastery (a fifth was too delicate to be opened then) now constitute the finest material available for study of these documents. This is especially so because the originals have faded from exposure despite the best of care under controlled conditions.

Sowmy left. Trever soon determined that what he had copied was a portion of Isaiah 65. Was the rest of Isaiah on that scroll? Could it be as old as the Nash Papyrus? Early the next morning Trever determined to go to St. Mark's in spite of the danger. With the aid of the Arab secretary of the school, he secured the necessary permissions and, risking life and limb, was taken by Miss Faris through the narrow, hazardous streets to the Syrian monastery. There he met the Metropolitan, who was at length convinced the manuscripts should again be brought to the school, where there were photographic equipment and better conditions for obtaining good results than in St. Mark's dim library.

Subsequent excavations at the caves indicated that the scrolls had been damaged when they were removed from their jars and unwrapped. Fragments from the manuscripts were on the floor of the cave. The documents had also been stripped of their linen protection and carried about in sacks, paper and otherwise. But at last the precious scrolls were in loving hands. Before returning them to St. Mark's, they were carefully wrapped. The seriously deteriorated leather scroll was placed in a specially constructed box. While this was going on, Trever sent photographic copies to the doyen of Palestinian archaeologists and the leading expert on ancient forms of writing, William F. Albright.

In the following days, Trever, sometimes accompanied by Burrows, now returned, made numerous trips to St. Mark's, each journey fraught with its own several perils. At least once the scrolls were returned to the American School. Trever was not pleased with all of his initial pictures. Ever a perfectionist in matters photographic, he wished to retake the Isaiah Scroll. This involved a difficult search of the shops of the city for proper film. Only outdated portrait film was located, but Trever rejoiced to find even this.

On March 15 a letter from Albright reached the school:

> *My heartiest congratulations on the greatest manuscript discovery of modern times! There is no doubt in my mind that the script is more archaic than that of the Nash Papyrus. ... I should prefer a date around 100 B.C.! What an absolutely incredible find! And there can happily not be the slightest doubt in the world about the genuineness of the manuscript.*

Within several weeks, steadily increasing violence forced the abandonment of the American School, with Trever the last to go. Samuel, under various urgings, sought a safe place for the scrolls; the monastery was a particularly vulnerable location. Sowmy suggested a bank vault in Beirut as

a safer place (shortly thereafter Sowmy was killed by bomb fragments as he stood in the courtyard at St. Mark's). Thus Beirut became the way station for the manuscripts on their journey to America.

The intriguing story of the scrolls in America cannot be told in detail here. Suffice it to say that Burrows, Trever, and Brownlee were able to continue their work on the texts and to publish them. Now famous, the Dead Sea Scrolls were displayed at various locations in the United States and seen by thousands. The publicity enhanced their value, but the Metropolitan's attempts to sell were clouded by claims to the scrolls by the new nations, Jordan and Israel, as well as the go-between Anton Kiraz. Confusion over ownership was such that Yale and Duke universities found reasons not to buy the scrolls. The Library of Congress displayed the scrolls but showed little interest in purchasing them. At last they came to rest in a specially prepared safe in the home of a Syrian Orthodox Christian in Worcester, Massachusetts.

Meanwhile, all scholars did not agree with the judgment of Albright and that of a vast and growing host. Tovia Wechsler, a journalist and something of a Hebraist, who had been one of the first to see the scrolls and who at the time had laughed them away, attacked Trever for his views and stoutly maintained that the story of the find was a hoax. Not only the manuscripts were under attack. Metropolitan Samuel was declared an outlaw in Jordan and found his integrity and

INSPIRATION FOR QUMRAN

This scroll of Isaiah, found in Cave 1, contains portions of about 30 chapters—approximately one-half of the book. It has been suggested that the founding of the community at Qumran was inspired by the words of Isaiah 40:3, "In the wilderness prepare the way of the Lord...."

reputation a matter of widespread debate. He decided to sell the scrolls by whatever means at hand. One way was a simple newspaper ad, which appeared in *The Wall Street Journal* on June 1, 1954.

On July 1, after delicate negotiations, the scrolls, accompanied by the Metropolitan and two others, came to the Waldorf Astoria Hotel in New York. There they met Mr. Sidney Esteridge, the would-be purchaser, with his lawyers and several experts. The price, $250,000, had been agreed upon in advance. It was a bargain by any realistic standard. After considerable discussion of various details in the bill of sale, the matter was consummated. Three months later the "Archbishop Samuel Trust" to aid Syrian Orthodox churches was considerably enriched. But the legal papers for the trust were not properly drawn. The sum was reported as personal income and the United States Internal Revenue Service got most of the purchase price.

For all the Archbishop knew the scrolls were in the private collection of a rich American. In February 1955 the Israeli prime minister announced that these four manuscripts were in Israel. How the scrolls came into the possession of the State of Israel remained somewhat of a mystery until Professor Yigael Yadin told the story. He tells how, on a visit to America, his attention was called to the newspaper ad. He knew the value of the materials and remembered the agonizing attempt of his father, Professor Sukenik, to obtain the scrolls in January of 1948. Yadin determined to try to buy the documents for the State of Israel. A direct approach was unwise. Thus a subterfuge was invented. Mr. Esteridge was in fact acting on behalf of Yadin and the Israeli government.

The four scrolls formerly in Metropolitan Samuel's possession thus were returned to Jerusalem to be with other major scrolls from Cave 1 at Qumran. They came to Hebrew University, which Professor Sukenik had honored with his knowledge for so long. But it was too late for Sukenik. He had died a year earlier. Now it is time to tell his part in the story.

On Sunday, November 23, 1947, Sukenik received a message from Faidi Salahi, a friend of Sukenik's and a dealer in antiquities. He had something of interest to show the scholar. The next morning, according to the professor's dramatic account, the two met across one of the barbed-wire barricades the British were erecting in an effort to keep violent factions apart.

The Armenian held up a scrap of leather. On it were Hebrew characters that Sukenik immediately recognized as being similar to those he had seen on early Jewish funeral urns. For the briefest moment he thought it must be a forgery of some sort. He had never heard of this kind of script on leather, parchment, or papyrus other than the Nash. But the man holding it was an old and trusted friend, and the fragment had all the appearances of authenticity. There and then he made up his mind to buy the document from which it came. Could other fragments be seen? Yes, said the Armenian, they were in Bethlehem. Could they be brought to Jerusalem? Yes.

On Thursday Sukenik, now armed with a pass allowing him through the barricades, went to his friend's shop and viewed additional pieces of the manuscript. He was convinced. He had to go to Bethlehem and deal directly with the Arab dealer who had the document in his possession. For Sukenik to visit an Arab area involved great personal risk. Moreover, the very next day the United Nations was scheduled to vote on the partition of Palestine. Whichever way the vote went, wholesale hostilities were almost sure to follow. His wife and his son, Yigael, then com-

On June 1, 1954, a modest advertisement in *The Wall Street Journal* announced that the scrolls had surfaced again.

mander of Jewish armed forces, knew the danger and argued against it. Persuasion put off the fulfillment of an archaeologist's dream. Then the U.N. delayed its vote. Jerusalem held its breath. It was an opening for Sukenik. The day was November 29, 1948.

There is a good deal of confusion about the events of that day with reference to the Dead Sea Scrolls. According to one story, Sukenik risked his life by going to Arab Bethlehem. There, according to this version, he was shown three scrolls and even allowed to bring them back to Jerusalem. According to another account, an Arab friend of the professor's brought them to him in Jerusalem. No matter. The net result is the same. Sukenik came into possession of three scrolls, which turned out to be the War Scroll, the Thanksgiving Scroll, and another copy of Isaiah in somewhat poorer condition than the magnificent Isaiah manuscript at St. Mark's.

The day after these ancient Hebrew scrolls came to Hebrew University, the United Nations voted to partition Palestine. Much moved by both events, Sukenik felt there was something symbolic in the coincidence. Full of joy at the acquisition of the documents, the professor told almost anyone who would listen of his good fortune. About a week later he told one of the university librarians. In astonished silence Sukenik listened to a tale this man had to relate. Some months before, he and another of the library staff had gone to St. Mark's Monastery in the Old City to have a look at some manuscripts. The Syrian Metropolitan wanted to know their content and age and whether Hebrew University might wish to acquire them. They were written in Samaritan, the two librarians decided, and were not very old. A little later he had called St. Mark's with the offer of a Samaritan specialist, but Samuel was away. Consequently, the matter was dropped.

Stunned, Sukenik could not believe what he was being told. Those so-called Samaritan manuscripts

were part of the collection he now had, he was sure of it. His impulse was to go by St. Mark's on his way home, but the Old City was now securely in Arab hands, and no one entered without a pass. This he was not likely to get, since his son was who he was. Even if by some miracle he got a pass, he had no money to offer for the scrolls.

Sukenik went home and began work on trying to raise funds. Slowly from various sources a little money

This aerial view of the Qumran terrace shows the buildings of Khirbet Qumran after excavation. The cliffs, where many of the scroll caves are located, rise above the terrace.

Professor Sukenik was the first scholar to set eyes on a fragment of the scrolls. He is credited with single-handedly returning to Jerusalem the War Scroll, the Thanksgiving Psalms Scroll, and the second of the two Isaiah scrolls.

began to accumulate. Sukenik thought that about £1,500 (then about $6,075) might be enough. Efforts to reach the Syrian priest and open negotiations came to nothing. Then, near the end of January, a letter came from the Old City from a man on whose property Sukenik had excavated an early Jewish tomb some years before. His name was Anton Kiraz. He offered to show some scrolls that were for sale. The rest of the story you know.

WHERE THE LOST WAS FOUND

CAVE 1, GENERAL VIEW, LIMESTONE CLIFFS

Many caves pock the steep limestone hills north of 'Ain Feshkha along the shore of the Dead Sea. In one of the most inconspicuous caves, shown here in the highlighted area, a remarkable discovery was made early in 1947, after which the small cavity would forever be called "Cave 1"—the cave where the first Dead Sea Scrolls were found.

MORE SCROLLS LIE BURIED!

Recollections from Years Gone By

By Baruch Safrai

With so much public attention lately focused on the Dead Sea Scrolls, the question is frequently asked, with increasing insistence: Are there more scrolls—either undiscovered in the caves or in the hands of the Bedouin or of those who acquired them from the Bedouin? This article will suggest that the answer is yes on both counts.

My story begins in 1953, when I joined an archaeological team led by the late Yohanan Aharoni to explore some caves in the Judean Desert near the Dead Sea. In 1947 Ta'amireh Bedouin had discovered the first of the now-famous Dead Sea Scroll caves in the vicinity of the Wadi Qumran. Once the Bedouin realized the financial rewards that could be realized from scroll materials, many of them turned from shepherding to cave exploring. In 1951 the Bedouin again hit paydirt, so to speak. They found more scrolls and other documents, albeit all fragmentary, in the Wadi Murabba'at, the wadi, or canyon, just south of the Wadi Qumran.

Both the Wadi Qumran and the Wadi Murabba'at were in territory then controlled by Jordan (now referred to as the West Bank). The Israeli border lay barely five miles south of the Wadi Murabba'at. This border, however, was no barrier to the Bedouin; they would regularly cross it with ease. In the summer of 1952, additional scrolls came on the antiquities market that supposedly had come from an "unknown source," but it was widely rumored that they came from caves within Israel. The Israel Department of Antiquities (now the Israel Antiquities Authority) quickly organized a survey of the area just south of the border, in the Judean desert, led by Aharoni, then an inspector for the department and later one of Israel's most distinguished archaeologists. I was a member of this team. From November 25 to December 16, 1953, we surveyed, among others, the Nahal Hever (*nahal* is the Hebrew for the Arabic wadi), from where these fragmentary texts from an "unknown source" had been rumored to have come.

In this area the cliffs rise about 1,500 feet above the Dead Sea, cut only by the wadis where the caves are located. The only way to reach these nearly inaccessible caves in the wadi walls is—and, especially at that time, was—from above. But even from above the task was difficult. There were no roads on the cliffs. To get to the caves, we often had to let ourselves down and up on ropes and rope ladders. Fortunately, we had assistance from the Israeli army. Equipment and food was brought in by hand or by mule.

Qumran's Cave of Horrors

Two Roman camps, one north and one south of the Nahal Hever, were discovered by the 1953 expedition. The southern camp, shown here, overlooks the Cave of Horrors, so named because of the dozens of skeletons found inside. The Roman camps date to the Second Jewish Revolt against Rome (also known as the Bar-Kokhba Revolt) of 132–135 C.E.; the skeletons are presumably those of Jewish refugees killed when the Romans camped above discovered their cave refuge.

Our most important find was the remains of two previously unknown Roman military camps, both on the cliffs above the caves. One was north and the other south of the Nahal Hever; both were used by the Romans when they laid siege to Jews hiding in the caves. Both camps overlooked the canyon, and both were above caves that later proved to be extremely rich in finds. The Roman camps dated to the time of the Second Jewish Revolt against Rome (132–135 C.E.). The camp on the south overlooked the cave later known as the Cave of Horrors, because it contained dozens of skeletons—men, women, and children, apparently Jewish refugees who had been cut off by the Romans from the camp they had built above the caves.

The camp on the north overlooked what later became known as the Cave of Letters. Because for ten years I had been a fisherman, I was given the task of securing the rope ladder we dropped down from above in order to reach the cave. It took me two days just to tie and aim the ladder; the ladder being over 300 feet long, I knew it had to be secure. In order to reach the Cave of Letters, someone had to descend almost 50 feet by foot along a dangerous path and then climb up the face of a wall from a small ledge, pulling a 60-foot rope ladder after him. In this way we were able to enter one of the two openings of a huge cave containing three different chambers.

The first thing we noticed was that the Bedouin had been there before us. Tell-tale signs of recent digging were evident throughout the cave—including empty cigarette packs from Jordan. We retrieved what ancient remains we could, fragments that were apparently regarded as worthless by the Bedouin—mostly broken pottery, some small pieces of cloth and mats and three lids, one made of clay, one of wood, and the third made of stone. This third lid had the Hebrew letter *shin,* which stands for *Shaddai* (Almighty), one of the Hebrew names of God. Unfortunately, this was not enough for Aharoni to decide whether the cave had been occupied during the two most likely periods: during the First (66–70 C.E.) or the Second Jewish Revolt against Rome, the so-called Bar-Kokhba Revolt (132–135 C.E.). Alas, sometimes Aharoni had no *mazel* (luck).

Six years later additional documents appeared on the antiquities market, once again from an "unknown source." This time the rumor was that they had come from a wadi farther south (Nahal Se'elim in Hebrew, Wadi Sieyal in Arabic)—deeper into Israel, even though they were offered for sale in Jordan. Again the Bedouin were ignoring the border, but with greater daring. The response was another Israeli archaeological expedition. It was divided into four teams, each of which explored adjacent wadis, descending into the caves from the cliffs above. Aharoni led one team, and his rival Yigael Yadin led another (the other two teams were led by Pesach Bar-Adon and Nahman Avigad). Aharoni chose the area that included the northern side of the Nahal Se'elim, where the most recent finds were said to have come from and where he found some fragmentary documents. Yadin was left with the area that included the northern side of the Nahal Hever. Nothing much was expected there because the area had already been explored seven years earlier by the Aharoni team. However, during two campaigns—one in March and April 1960 and a second in March 1961—Yadin's team made some extraordinary discoveries in this cave: a fragment from the book of Psalms, a fragment from the book of Numbers, a cache of documents now known as the Babata archive,[1] glass, mats, metal vessels, ancient keys with which they locked their homes when fleeing from the Romans, and, most exciting, the Bar-Kokhba

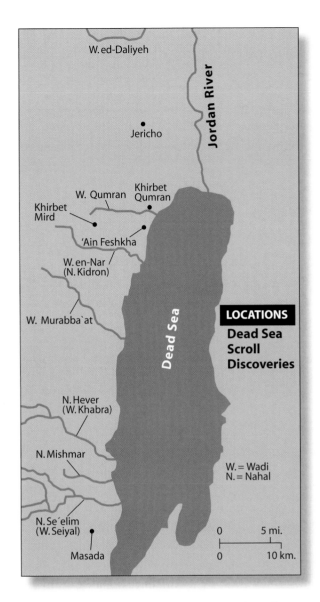

W. ed-Daliyeh

Jordan River

Jericho

W. Qumran

Khirbet Qumran

Khirbet Mird

'Ain Feshkha

W. en-Nar (N. Kidron)

W. Murabba'at

Dead Sea

LOCATIONS
Dead Sea Scroll Discoveries

N. Hever (W. Khabra)

N. Mishmar

W. = Wadi
N. = Nahal

N. Se'elim (W. Seiyal)

Masada

0   5 mi.

0   10 km.

letters (letters from the files of Bar-Kokhba's military command, including some from and to Bar-Kokhba himself). Because of the Babata archive and the Bar-Kokhba letters, the cave became known as the Cave of Letters.

Have Ladder, Will Travel

The rugged and steep terrain near the Dead Sea made the caves within the cliffs accessible only by rope ladder. Author Safrai, thanks to ten years of experience as a fisherman, was given the task of securing the 300-foot rope ladder that was used to reach the Cave of Horrors. Reaching the Cave of Letters required a 60-foot rope ladder

THE CAVE OF LETTERS

Despite having been explored by Israeli archaeologist Yohanan Aharoni in 1953, the Cave of Letters (highlighted area) yielded remarkable new finds in 1960 to a team led by Yigael Yadin, Israel's most famous archaeologist and military commander and Aharoni's professional rival. The discoveries included fragments from the book of Psalms, a fragment from the book of Numbers, a cache of legal documents, and letters from Bar-Kokhba's military command, including some to and from Bar-Kokhba himself.

SCROLLS—AND SKELETONS

In 1953 Baruch Safrai wedged himself between fallen boulders within the Cave of Letters and discovered a human skeleton pinned under the boulders. The skeleton was still clothed in a white robe, with a rope belt, knotted in front, around the waist. The first-century Jewish historian Josephus records that the Essenes would give initiates "a girdle and a white garment."

Some of the documents in the Babata archive bore internal dates to the second century C.E., the time of the Second Jewish Revolt and the years immediately prior to that. The Bar-Kokhba letters were obviously from the same period.

Yadin carefully noted the findspot of the small fragment from the book of Psalms: "near the passage from hall A to hall B." He surmised that the fragment had fallen from a possibly intact scroll that the Bedouin had removed from the cave. "We may assume that it actually belonged to a scroll found by the Bedouins and was torn off when they crawled out," he wrote.[2] This scroll has never turned up. One wonders if it is still out there in the hands of some antiquities dealer or an "investor." That is why I said at the beginning of this article that there may well be other scrolls in the hands of the Bedouin or those who obtained them from the Bedouin.

In Yadin's second campaign to the Cave of Letters (in 1961), he had found the fragment from the book of Numbers.[3] In addition, Yadin found some papyrus fragments from other documents. Again Yadin surmised that "The Bedouin who ransacked the cave had evidently left by this opening, dropping these fragments

on their way out." "We may assume," he concluded, "as in the case of the fragment of Psalms found in the first season, that larger pieces of this scroll are now in Jordan."[4] Like the Psalms scroll, however, the scroll of the book of Numbers has not yet appeared—if it was ever retrieved by the Bedouin.

But we can do nothing about that. The more insistent, if no less tantalizing, question is whether there is a lower stratum in the Cave of Letters. In the exposed areas of the cave, it is clear that the Bedouin had already rummaged around and presumably extracted whatever may have been there. If there was anything left, Aharoni and Yadin would have found it.

There are certain areas in the cave, however, where neither Yadin, Aharoni, nor the Bedouin could have reached. In the three chambers of the cave are huge piles of boulders that had fallen from the roof of the cave; Yadin correctly assumed that these collapses had occurred, "in the main, before the time of Bar-Kokhba."[5] The roof of the cave in chamber B is approximately 30 feet above the floor. The pile of boulders that fell from the roof is nearly 20 feet high. You can imagine what a pile of stones it is! Even Yadin conceded in 1962 that "We could not move the enormous blocks of fallen rock"[6]—even with the use of hydraulic hammers. They simply "examined all the cracks and cavities and also removed the small and medium-sized stones."[7] The investigation was thus limited to what was accessible.

Aharoni's team had tried eight years earlier to move several of the boulders at the edge of the pile, but we succeeded in only a few cases; the boulders were simply too large. Moreover, the entire pile of boulders was covered by bat dung. Every time we moved a boulder, we stirred up a cloud of acrid dust that made it difficult to breathe. But I was young and slim and lithe in those days, and strong in the bargain. I offered to try to shift some of the boulders and wriggle in among the gaps. I climbed up about halfway on the west side of the pile in chamber B[8] and shifted a few of the boulders. Then I began to descend snakelike in among the gaps, with my arms thrust forward, shining a powerful flashlight ahead of me.

When I had penetrated down to about the length of my body, I glimpsed by the light of the flashlight, pinned under the boulders, a human skeleton lying on its side with its arms and legs asprawl. The skeleton was clothed in a white robe. Around the waist was a rope belt, knotted in front.

The discovery of this skeleton made a powerful impression on me that remains vivid to this day. Of course I could not see the entire skeleton, only those parts that were visible under the glare of my flashlight through the gaps in the boulders.

I immediately reported the discovery to Aharoni, who rushed back into the chamber carrying a few padded cardboard boxes. I again wriggled down among the boulders and described to Aharoni what I was able to see: the skeleton, the posture, the clothing. He instructed me to remove whatever I could. I strained, painfully squeezing between the boulders, gasping for breath. Finally I managed to reach the middle part of the skeleton. I pulled away the rope belt and part of the robe. Once I reached them, they were easy to pull out; apparently the underside of the robe and the belt beneath the skeleton had disintegrated. I was unable to get any of the bones, however.

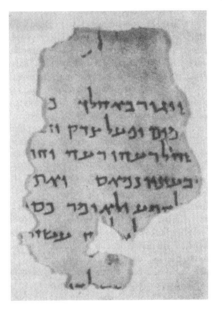

This fragment of parts of Psalm 15 and the beginning of Psalm 16 is dated to the latter half of the first century C.E. Baruch Safrai is convinced more spectacular finds wait to be discovered under the boulders that are inside the various caves overlooking the Dead Sea.

When I emerged from the maze of boulders covered with dust and bat dung, I presented Aharoni with the piece of the robe and the belt. I remember the thought that flashed through my mind after discussing the find with Aharoni. Josephus, the first-century Jewish historian, tells how the Essenes would give an initiate "a girdle and a white garment." I pictured my "Essene" walking about dressed in the white robe and belt I handed to Aharoni. "He will perpetually be a lover of truth … [and will never] endeavor to outshine his subjects, either in his garments or any other finery," wrote Josephus.[9]

Aharoni placed the robe and belt in a cardboard box. Today no one knows where they are. My effort to find them in the stores of the Antiquities Authority proved fruitless. It may be that they never reached Jerusalem; I recall that one of the boxes containing finds, which was carried to our base camp at Ein Gedi by the IDF soldiers who were helping us, did not get there and was either lost, stolen, or forgotten on the way.

The implications of this robe and rope are vitally significant. The position of the skeleton under the boulders clearly indicates that this was no ordinary burial; the skeleton lay sprawled out, apparently crushed when the roof of the cave collapsed. All the other datable finds capable of distinguishing between the First and Second Revolts were found on top of the collapse, not beneath it. This proves there is something from an earlier period under the pile of boulders: there is definitely a lower stratum. The Bedouin knew this. They dug some tunnels under the piles of boulders; apparently they had discovered something and were looking for more. As Aharoni noted in his report, "We noticed that the Bedouin had dug several small, narrow tunnels and had crawled between the piles of stones; they were, however, unable to move them. There was no possibility of a proper archaeological excavation."[10]

Several Israeli expeditions in the 1950s and early 1960s uncovered spectacular finds—including caches of letters, biblical fragments, even a white-robed skeleton—but the difficulties in excavating inside almost inaccessible caves prevented thorough investigation.

I should add that Aharoni was fully aware of the importance of the stratum beneath the pile of boulders. In his published report he noted that "all of the central chamber and most of the last one—where the bones were found—could not be properly explored and excavated owing to the heavy rock-falls covering the floor.... The few days available to the expedition were not enough to thoroughly research this large cave and clear up the problem of dating and period of its occupation. A great deal of research work, including overcoming the technical difficulties involved in removing the piled-up boulders from the cave's floor, still awaits the expedition over the next few years."[11]

As noted above, Yadin, too, was aware of the problem posed by the rockfalls.[12] It is clear that we now have the time and the technical ability to remove these large piles of rocks and carefully excavate underneath them.

But the Cave of Letters is not the only cave that should be reexcavated. The reason relates to the cause of the roof collapse in the Cave of Letters. I consulted a geologist from the Israel Geological Institute who studies ancient earthquakes, Dr. J. Kurtz, who

explained to me that, theoretically, there were three possible causes of the roof collapse in the Cave of Letters: (1) fatigue of the stone in the roof—areas with minor cracks finally broke loose—what geologists call progressive fissuring; (2) water cutting the roof area away; and (3) earthquake.

The first two would be local phenomena. The third, earthquake, would affect other caves as well. This is an area of relatively frequent earthquakes. The Jordan Valley, the Dead Sea (the lowest spot on earth), and the Arabah (the valley south of the Dead Sea) are all part of the Great Rift that extends through the Red Sea into Africa. It marks the edge of two tectonic plates that, in geological terms, rather frequently rub up against one another, causing earthquakes.[13]

According to Dr. Kurtz, ten to fifteen relatively strong earthquakes occurred in this region in the 300-year period from about 250 B.C.E. to 70 C.E., when most scholars date the Dead Sea Scrolls associated with the Wadi Qumran. One of these earthquakes is especially famous. We know precisely when it occurred: in the seventh year of Herod's reign, according to Josephus.[14] This places it in the year 31 B.C.E.

Archaeologists have used this earthquake in 31 B.C.E. to explain the destruction and temporary abandonment of an early settlement at Qumran. They have also used it to explain the destruction of the Herodian palaces near Jericho, a few miles north of Qumran. It is tempting to attribute the collapse of the roof in the Cave of Letters to this same earthquake, but only renewed excavations can test this hypothesis.

More intriguing still, archaeological reports are replete with references to other caves in this area whose roofs have collapsed. For example, in Pesach Bar-Adon's report of his 1960 survey of caves in the Judean desert, he states: "We investigated tens of caves ... several large and deep ones, their floors covered by large rock-falls."[15] In one cave Bar-Adon found two scroll fragments, one in Greek and the other in Hebrew. The Hebrew one, he says, "was found near a later rock-fall." Bar-Adon then adds: "Perhaps the missing part of the complete scroll is yet pinned under these rocks."[16] I need only add that Bar-Adon also found pottery in these caves dating to the first century B.C.E. and earlier. In a 1970 return to the same area, Bar-Adon reports that in a "large number of caves, the floors are covered with huge rocks."[17] In

short, it appears that the ceiling collapses in the caves were a result of earthquakes, or perhaps one major earthquake, that buried artifacts and perhaps scrolls from the period before the Roman destruction of the temple (70 C.E.).

Most of the eleven caves in the area of the Wadi Qumran containing inscriptional material were discovered by Bedouin, not by archaeologists. One of the few exceptions was Cave 3. The most intriguing find from Cave 3 is the famous Copper Scroll, the only scroll from antiquity that is inscribed on metal. Over 7.5 feet long, the Copper Scroll is a list of sixty-four hiding places of huge amounts of gold and silver. Many scholars believe it is a guide to where the temple treasure was hidden to prevent its capture by the Romans.[18] Cave 3 was found by archaeologists instead of Bedouin because the mouth of the cave was blocked by large stones that had fallen from the roof, probably as a result of an earthquake. The Copper Scroll also mentions a second copy of directions to this buried treasure. Does it lie buried in some nearby cave under a pile of rocks? While some scholars believe the Copper Scroll is a roadmap to real buried treasure, others believe the inventory is entirely fictional—none of the locations has ever been discovered, despite numerous amateur efforts to do so. Perhaps this debate will never be settled. But the one way it could be settled is if one of the treasure spots were found with the treasure still intact.

WE HAVEN'T SEEN THE LAST OF THE SCROLLS

Kibbutznik Baruch Safrai is not the only one who believes that additional scrolls lie undiscovered in collapsed caves. This view is shared by many scholars, including two of the most prominent members of the original publication team, Professor Frank Moore Cross of Harvard University and Professor John Strugnell, also of Harvard University and formerly chief editor of the scroll publication team. Both men expressed themselves on a recently released video entitled "The Enigma of the Dead Sea Scrolls."

"I think I can say there are still scrolls, mostly in collapsed caves," said Cross. "One day these will come to light. It will be very exciting!"

Strugnell noted that "every 25 years or so, the Jordan Valley is torn apart by earthquakes. That's when I expect old collapsed caves to be opened. That's when I expect certain manuscripts to come to light."

As Safrai points out, however, we don't need to wait for an earthquake to recover what may still lie undiscovered in some of the caves.

WHO IS BARUCH SAFRAI?

Safrai was born in Jerusalem in 1926. While a youth he joined the HaShomer HaTzair (Young Guards) movement, which advocated national self-fulfillment and self-reliance. After Israel's War of Independence in 1948. Safrai settled in Kibbutz Sa'ar, along the country's northern coast and near the biblical port of Achziv. The kibbutz became a fishing and agricultural settlement.

Safrai worked as a fisherman for nearly ten years. His interest in archaeology was kindled by the ancient pottery that the kibbutz fishing boats would periodically pull up in their nets. In 1990 Safrai earned a B.A. in archaeology from Haifa University and wrote a pamphlet on marine archaeology called "About Jars and the Sea." His interests led him to serve as an assistant to the late Yohanan Aharoni, one of Israel's leading archaeologists

Safrai has not had far to go for some of his discoveries. Underneath the fields of his kibbutz he has uncovered an ancient agricultural site and a Byzantine house with a colorful mosaic and a plaster floor (the latter was published in an Israeli archaeology periodical). He established and continues to tend the kibbutz collection of the ancient pottery hauled up by members and its collection of coins and flint and petrified objects.

Safrai has been active for decades years in Chug L'Yediat HaAretz (Knowledge of the Land Group), a society he helped found that is devoted to promoting knowledge of Israel's history, archaeology, and geology. He has also published articles on those subjects. In addition, he is an experienced schoolteacher.

Never one to stay in a rut, Safrai's recent challenge is growing commercial roses in the kibbutz hothouses and conducting horticultural experiments at Hebrew University's agriculture facility. (Some of his experiments have been published in agriculture journals as articles with titles like "Increasing the Yield of Roses by Incision.") Safrai keeps a hand in fishing by working in the relatively new field of aquaculture, the practice of raising fish in enclosed waters. As if all that were not enough, Safrai spends the remainder of his workweek in the kibbutz industrial factory.

One more thing—Safrai teaches Hebrew to recently arrived immigrants from the former Soviet Union. Once a pioneer, always a pioneer.—Steven Feldman

What more likely place than in an inaccessible cave guarded by a rockfall from an ancient earthquake?

It is evident that the collapsed roof in the Cave of Letters makes a clean division between two occupational strata inside the cave, the first one underneath the fallen boulders, hiding, perhaps, the signs of an earlier Essene occupation. In my opinion, this may also be true of other caves in the Judean Desert whose roofs collapsed, perhaps in the same earthquake.

For all these reasons—practical and visionary—excavation under the boulders of roof collapses in these caves is mandatory. Today we have the equipment and the know-how to accomplish it. All we need is the will and the financial support. And there is no better place to start than the Cave of Letters, where, over fifty years ago, I saw a skeleton clothed in a white robe and a rope belt pinned under the stones.

This article is dedicated to the memory of Professor Yohanan Aharoni, a friend to everyone and to me.

Acknowledgments

My thanks to Professor Avraham Ronen of Haifa University for his advice and help with the presentation of this article. I am also grateful to Dr. Beno Rothenberg (who took part in the expedition) for his help and encouragement and to Dr. Bilha Nitzan. I also gratefully acknowledge the help of archaeologist Nurit Faig and Tamar Shik.

NOTES

1. Babata was a Jewish woman from a village on the shore of the Dead Sea who fled to the cave with her family's legal documents during the Second Jewish Revolt. See Joseph A. Fitzmyer's review of *The Documents from the Bar Kokhba Period in the Cave of Letters: Greek Papyri,* edited by Naphtali Lewis, *Biblical Archaeology Review* (May-June 1990).

2. Yigael Yadin, *Bar-Kokhba* (New York: Random House, 1971), 114.

3. Yadin, "Expedition D—The Cave of the Letters," *Israel Exploration Journal* 12 (1962): 227–29.

4. Yadin, "Expedition D," 228.

5. Yadin, "Expedition D," 230.

6. Yadin, "Expedition D," 231.

7. Yadin, "Expedition D," 231.

8. Yohanan Aharoni and Beno Rothenberg, *In the Footsteps of Kings and Rebels* (Ramat-Gan, Israel: Massada, 1960), 130–32 (in Hebrew). In Aharoni's report he indicates that it was found in chamber c. Because of this discrepancy I have tried to consult the original handwritten diary that Aharoni kept of the expedition but have not yet been able to do so. If Aharoni's field notes state that the find was in chamber c, I will accept this correction.

9. Josephus, *The Jewish War* 2.8.

10. Yohanan Aharoni, "The Caves of Nahal Hever," *Atiqot* 3 (1961): 153–55.

11. Aharoni, "Caves of Nahal Hever," 153–55, 161.

12. Yigael Yadin, *Finds from the Bar-Kokhba Period in The Cave of Letters* (Jerusalem: Israel Exploration Society, 1963), 17 (in Hebrew).

13. See Dan Gill's review of Amos Nur's video, "Earthquakes in the Holy Land," *Biblical Archaeology Review* (September-October 1991).

14. Josephus, *Jewish Antiquities* 15.5, 2; *The Jewish War* 1.15, 3.

15. "Judean Desert-Caves Archaeology Survey in 1960," *Yediot* (Bulletin of the Israel Exploration Society) 25 A-B (1961) (in Hebrew).

16. "Judean Desert-Caves," 36.

17. Pesach Bar-Adon, "Excavations in the Judean Desert," *Atiqot* 9, Hebrew Series (1989).

18. See P. Kyle McCarter Jr., "The Mysterious Copper Scroll: Clues to Hidden Temple Treasure?" *Bible Review* (August 1992).

A

EXCAVATING A NEW ENTRANCE

Viewed from the terrace directly south of the Qumran buildings, the entrance to Cave 4 can be seen on the side of the marl rib of the terrace wall jutting out to the south (inset A) over the wadi floor below.

When excavations began in the cave, an upper, more convenient entrance was cut into the chalky marl. The new entrance is visible just above and to the right of the original entrance (inset B).

THE DEAD SEA SCROLLS AND THE PEOPLE WHO WROTE THEM

By Frank Moore Cross

After decades of discovery and publication, the study of the manuscripts from the desert of Judah has entered a new, more mature phase. True, the heat and noise of the early controversies have not wholly dissipated. One occasionally hears the agonized cry of a scholar pinned beneath a collapsed theory. And in the popular press, no doubt, the so-called battle of the scrolls will continue to be fought with mercenaries for some time to come. However, the initial period of confusion is past. From the burgeoning field of scroll research and the new disciplines it has created, certain coherent patterns of fact and meaning have emerged.

The scrolls and the people who wrote them can be placed within a broad historical framework with relative certainty by virtue of external controls provided by the archaeologist and the paleographer. At that point, the historian must begin a difficult task—difficult because internal data from the scrolls pose special historiographic problems resulting from their esoteric language. The usual methods of historical criticism are difficult to apply without excessive subjectivity.

The archaeological context of the community of the Dead Sea—its caves, community center, and agricultural adjunct at 'Ain Feshkha—has been established by six major seasons of excavations. The ancient center has yielded a clear stratification, and in turn the strata are closely dated by their yield of artifacts, notably coins. For the era in which we are especially interested, the site exhibits three phases. The first of these, so-called Period Ia, consists of the remains of the earliest communal structures. In Period Ib the settlement was almost completely rebuilt and enlarged. The coins suggest that the buildings of the second phase were constructed no later than the time of Alexander Jannaeus (103–76 B.C.E.). The dating of the first phase is more difficult. So thoroughly were the structures of the first phase rebuilt that only the barest foundations were left. The problem is further complicated by the relatively short life and small size of

Qumran's Unyielding Cliffs

From these various views of the marl ribs forming the terraces of Qumran's landscape, it is not hard to see why the cliffs were so reluctant to give up their secret scrolls or why the scrolls' excavation was a challenge that took many years to yield success.

the first phase; few coins accumulate in foundations in the first years of occupation. Moreover, coins have a considerable period of currency. When Alexander Jannaeus introduced the new Jewish coinage, coins of the Seleucid kings continued to circulate. The earliest coins of Period Ia appear to be five Seleucid coppers of imprecise date from the reign of Antiochus VII Sidetes (138–129 B.C.E.). This and other coin evidence indicates that the first buildings were probably constructed at the site Qumran sometime in the interval between 140 and 100 B.C.E.

In the second phase, Period Ib, the community center took its permanent form, though extensions or repairs of a minor sort were introduced before the destruction of its buildings in the earthquake of 31 B.C.E., reported by the first-century historian Josephus. After a short but indeterminate period of abandonment, the site was reoccupied, rebuilt, and repaired precisely on the plan of the old communal complex. It flourished until 68 C.E., when it was stormed and occupied by the forces of the Roman Emperor Vespasian in the course of his raid on Jericho.

Theoretically, I suppose, the communities occupying the ruins in each of these phases need not have been related.[1] In fact, the community of the second and third, and no doubt the little-known first phase, was one continuing community. It takes more than the historian's normally vivacious imagination to conceive of two communities, following one upon another and leading the peculiar life reflected at Qumran without having a relationship to one another. The very setting of the community requires a special explanation. Only powerful motivations would send a large group of persons into this wasteland. But more difficult to explain than the desolate environment chosen by the desert folk is the special character of the community center. The center was composed of communal facilities for study, writing, eating, domestic industries, and common stores. The members of the community did not live in the buildings (for the most part at any rate) but in caves and shelters radiating out from the central buildings. Thus, the architectural functions of the rooms and structures require a special mode of religious and communistic life. We can conclude only that the people of the scrolls founded the community in the second half of the century B.C.E. and occupied it, with a brief interruption in the reign of Herod the Great, until the dreadful days of the Jewish Revolt, which culminated in the Roman destruction of the Jewish State.

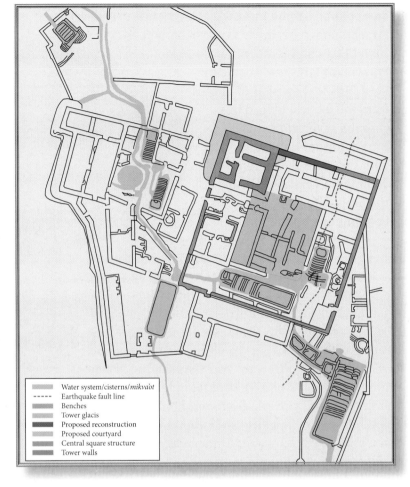

Water system/cisterns/*mikva'òt*
Earthquake fault line
Benches
Tower glacis
Proposed reconstruction
Proposed courtyard
Central square structure
Tower walls

Corroboration of this dating of the archaeological evidence is immediately furnished by the paleographical analysis of approximately six hundred manuscripts recovered from Qumran. The main lines of the evolution of the late Aramaic and early Jewish bookhands had already been fixed on the basis of documents and inscriptions analyzed between the two World Wars.[2] Now, thanks to the discoveries in the Judean desert, the science of early Jewish paleography has grown rich in materials for the typology of scripts.[3] These discoveries include not only the manuscripts of Qumran in paleo-Hebrew, Jewish, and Greek bookhands, but also the important discoveries from the Wadi Murabba'at and the Nahal Hever, written in both formal and cursive Jewish hands, as well as in Greek, Latin, and Nabatean. While these discoveries have occupied the center of the stage, other discoveries from the Wadi ed-Daliyeh north of Jericho, from the excavations of Khirbet Qumran, from the tombs of Jerusalem, from Khirbet el-Kom, and from the excavations at Masada, to mention only the most important, have steadily expanded, extending our knowledge of the evolution and relative dating of early Jewish scripts.

An Ancient Communal Café

A long room near the southern limits of the buildings was identified by the excavators as an assembly hall that also functioned as a communal dining hall. Visible at the far end of the hall was a flat stone that may have served as a podium from which a reader read to the group during meals.

Two columns of the Habakkuk Commentary (Pesher) appear here. A pesher is a type of early Jewish Biblical commentary that was not known until this scroll came to light. This text consists of quotes from the Biblical text, in this case the seventh-century B.C.E. prophet Habakkuk, with sentence-by-sentence commentaries showing how the Biblical text applies to the contemporary situation.

Not only do we now possess ample materials for precise typological analysis of the scripts of the Qumran manuscripts, but we have also accumulated a series of externally dated scripts by which the relative dates gained by typological study can be turned into absolute dates. Most striking no doubt are the documents bearing date formulae of the late fourth century B.C.E. (Daliyeh), of the third century (el-Kom), and of the first and second centuries of the Christian era (Qumran, Murabba'at, and Hever), which overlap in part and extend the Qumran series backward and forward in time. To these may be added documents from excavations, notably from Qumran itself and Masada, dated by archaeological context to the first century B.C.E. and later.

The scripts from Qumran belong to three periods of paleographical development. A very small group of Biblical manuscripts belong to an archaic style whose limits are about 250–150 B.C.E. Next, a large number of Qumran manuscripts, Biblical and non-Biblical, were written in a style reflecting the Hasmonean period, between 150 and 30 B.C.E. However, scrolls of specifically sectarian content, many composed and copied at Qumran, begin only about the middle of the Hasmonean period, about 100 B.C.E. Finally, there is a relatively large corpus of Herodian manuscripts dating between 30 B.C.E. and 70 C.E.

The termination of the series with late Herodian hands correlates precisely with the archaeological data. The library was abandoned at the time of the destruction of the community in 68 C.E. We must in turn establish the origins of the community no later

Old Scrolls — New Testament

When this scroll and fragments of other pesharim from Qumran were discovered, scholars noticed that this form of Jewish Biblical interpretation is reflected in the way quotations from the Hebrew Scriptures are sometimes treated in the New Testament. Examples can be found in the Gospels and in the letters of Paul and other early Christian writers. For examples of Christian pesharim, see Matthew 2:14–15, 16–18, and 23 and Galatians 3:6–7, 8–9, 13, and 16.

than the date of the earliest sectarian compositions, somewhat before 100 B.C.E. Nonsectarian scrolls, especially the Biblical manuscripts, begin in quantity about 150 B.C.E. Scrolls of the Archaic Period are exceedingly rare and were probably master scrolls brought into the community at the time of its founding. Extant copies of such characteristic sectarian scrolls as the Rule of the Community and the Damascus Document go back to the beginning of the first century B.C.E. Sectarian commentaries on Habakkuk, Nahum, and other Biblical works date mostly from the second half of the first century B.C.E. and contain traditional lore of Biblical interpretation developed in the community in its earlier history and precipitated into writing relatively late in the life of the sect.

Classical tests that treat the second century B.C.E. mention four Jewish movements in Judea; the Hasidim, a pious "congregation" that disappeared in the Maccabean era, and three orders that emerge no later than the early Hasmonean era and presumably have their roots in the Maccabean period. These are the Essenes, the Pharisees, and the Sadducees. Of these three, only the Essene order can be described as separatist, in the radical sense that they regarded themselves as the only true Israel and separated themselves fully from contact with their fellow Jews. Josephus informs us that the Essenes rejected even the sacrificial service of the temple as unclean and "offered their sacrifices by themselves." Pliny tells us of their "city" in the wilderness between Jericho and Ein Gedi near the shore of the Dead Sea—where the Qumran ruins are located.

This reference in Pliny is decisive in identifying the sectarians of Qumran with the Essenes, in the absence of strong counter-arguments. We know of no other sect arising in the second century B.C.E. which can be associated with the wilderness community. Surface exploration has turned up no rival settlement in the crucial era. Further, the community at Qumran was organized precisely as a new Israel, a true sect that repudiated the priesthood and cultus of Jerusalem. Neither the Pharisees nor the Sadducees can qualify. The Essenes qualify perfectly. The strongest argument that has been raised against the identification of the Qumran sect with the Essenes is as follows: since Palestine "swarmed" with obscure sects in the first century of the Christian era, one must exercise caution in assigning the Dead Sea sect to a known group. This argument had plausibility *only* when a few manuscripts of uncertain date were known.

The Qumran sect was not one of the small, ephemeral groups of the first century of the common era. Its substantial community at Qumran was established in the second century B.C.E. and flourished some two centuries or more. Moreover, it was not restricted to Qumran but, like the Essenes of the classical sources, counted its camps and settlements throughout the villages of Judah.

Its own sectarian literature was enormous, exercising a considerable influence upon later sectarian, including Christian, literature. The task, therefore, is to identify a major sect in Judaism. To suppose that a major group in Judaism in this period went unnoticed in our sources is simply incredible.

Scholars who "exercise caution" in identifying the sect of Qumran with the Essenes place themselves in an astonishing position: they must suggest seriously that two major parties formed communistic religious communities in the same district of the desert of the Dead Sea and lived

WHO WERE THE ESSENES?

For centuries, Essene communities dwelt on the shores of the Dead Sea. The Essenes, in the days of Philo and Josephus, were imbued with the utmost reverence for Moses and the law. They believed in God, the creator, in the immortality of the soul, and in a future state of retribution.

The Essenes' strict observance of purity laws compelled them to become a self-supporting community. They undertook various trades, cultivated their own fields, made all articles of dress and housewares, and avoided contact with those who did not observe the same rules. Essene daily life followed a strict pattern. They rose before the sun and were silent until they had assembled for prayers. Each then went to his appointed task. After a daily rite of baptism in cold water, they ate a common noon meal in silence. After working until evening, they again assembled for prayers and a common meal.

together in effect for two centuries, holding similar views and performing similar lustrations, ritual meals, and religious ceremonies. They must argue that the one carefully described by classical authors disappeared without leaving behind building remains or even potsherds and that the other, ignored by the classical sources, left extensive ruins and a great library. I prefer to flatly identify the men of Qumran

STUDY HALL 101

Two rooms near the scriptorium suggest a study hall and library. Low, plastered ledges lining the walls are suggestive of benches in early synagogues.

with their perennial house guests, the Essenes. At all events, in the remainder of this article I shall assume the identification and draw freely upon both classical and Qumran texts.

The Essenes of Qumran were a priestly party. Their leader was a priest. The archenemy of the sect was a priest, usually designated the Wicked Priest. In protocols of their community, the priests took precedence, and in the age to come a messiah priest ranked above the traditional Davidic or royal messiah. There is some reason to believe that the sect conducted a sacrificial system in its community at Qumran. At any rate, the community was preoccupied with priestly lore, ceremonial law, the orders of the priests, and the liturgical calendar; many of their sectarian compositions reflect an almost obsessive interest in orthodox priestly practice and observance.

The community referred to its priesthood as the "sons of Zadok," members of the ancient line of Biblical high priests. At the same time, they heaped scorn and bitter condemnation on the ungodly priests of Jerusalem, who, they argued, were illegitimate. This animosity toward the priests in power in Judah did not stem

merely from doctrinal differences but from a struggle for power between high-priestly families. The Essenes withdrew in defeat and formed their community in exile, which was organized as a counter-Israel led by a counter-priesthood or, viewed with Essene eyes, as the true Israel of God led by the legitimate priesthood. The theocrat of Jerusalem, the so-called Wicked Priest, attacked the Essene priesthood, even in exile, and made an attempt on the life of the Righteous Teacher, the Essene priestly leader. For their part, the Essene priests confidently expected divine intervention to establish their cause. They predicted that the Wicked Priest and his cronies would meet violent death at the hand of God and their enemies, and they searched Scripture for prophecies of the end of days when they, the poor of the desert, would be reestablished in a new, transfigured Jerusalem.

Another form in which written text was preserved at Qumran was in phylacteries (*tefillin*). Phylacteries held Biblical texts, including future prophecies foretold by God. This one was probably retrieved from Cave 4.

Mention of the Essene hopes of a new age of glory leads us naturally to some comments on the special theological views of the Essenes that informed their understanding of history and gave to their community its peculiar institutions. The Essenes belong in the center of that movement that goes under the designation *apocalypticism.* The late visionaries of the Old Testament, notably the author of Daniel, as well as the later John the Baptist and Christian communities, thought themselves to be living in the last days of the old age, or rather in the days when the old age was passing away and the kingdom of God was dawning. According to apocalypticism, the upsurge of evil powers in history reflected the last defiant outbreak of cosmic Satanic powers, and the gifts of the Holy Spirit, manifest in the community of the faithful, adumbrated the age of the Spirit to follow the final war in which the Spirit of Truth and his heavenly armies would put an end to the rule of the powers of darkness.

The constitution of the Essene community was a crystallized apocalyptic vision. Each institution and practice was a preparation for or, by anticipation, a realization of, life in the new age of God's rule. On the one hand, their communal life reenacted the events of the end time, both the final days of the old age and the era of Armageddon. On the other hand, their community, as heirs of the kingdom, participated already in the gifts and glories that were the first fruits of the age to come.

For the apocalyptist of Qumran, the key to these future mysteries was at hand. One had only to read Biblical prophecies with the understanding given the inspired interpreter (that is, one who reads under the power of the Holy Spirit), because the secrets of events to come in the last days were foretold by God through the mouth of his holy prophets. So the Essenes searched the Scriptures. They developed a body of traditional exegesis, no doubt inspired by patterns laid down by their founder, that is reflected in most of their works, above all in their Biblical commentaries, *pesharim,* in which their common tradition was fixed in writing.

In apocalyptic exegesis, three principles should be kept in mind. Prophecy openly or cryptically refers to the last days. Second, the so-called last days are in fact the present, the days of the sect's life. And, finally, the history of ancient Israel's redemption, its offices and institutions, are prototypes of the events and figures of the new Israel.

On this basis, the Essene camp in the wilderness found its prototype in the Mosaic camp of Numbers (see Numbers 2–4; 9:15–10:28). The Essenes retired to Qumran to "prepare the way of the Lord" in the wilderness. As God established his ancient covenant in the desert, so the Essenes entered into the new covenant on their return to the desert. As Israel in the desert was mustered into army ranks in preparation for the holy war of conquest, so the Essenes marshaled their community in battle array and wrote liturgies of

THE WAR SCROLL

The full title of this scroll from Cave 1 is "The War of the Sons of Light and the Sons of Darkness," which is often abbreviated as the "War Scroll." This sectarian document provides instructions for the anticipated forty-year war that God's righteous warriors (the Sons of Light) would fight at the end of the age against God's enemies (the Sons of Darkness). The document describes in detail preparations for war, the armaments to be worn, the carnage that will be inflicted, and the final victory against the *Kittim* (presumably the Romans). There are also specific instructions for the priests and Levites who will be in the camp, the blessing to be pronounced at the time of victory, and the thanksgiving ceremony. Fragmentary copies of this scroll were also found in Cave 4.

the holy warfare of Armageddon, living for the day of the second conquest when they would march with their messianic leaders to Zion. Meanwhile, they kept the laws of purity laid down in Scripture for soldiers in holy warfare, an ascetic regimen that at the same time anticipated life with the holy angels before the throne of God, a situation requiring similar ritual purity.

The sect's offices reveal this apocalyptic typology. The council of the community was numbered after the princes of Israel and Levi in the desert; at the same time, they prefigured the judges who would rule the tribes of Israel in the new age. As God sent Moses, Aaron, and David, so they looked for three messiahs: prophet, priest, and prince. The founder of their community bore a Biblical sobriquet, the "Righteous Teacher" (from Hosea 10:12 and Joel 2:23), apparently understood as the title of a priestly forerunner of the messianic age. And even the enemies of the sect, the False Oracle, the Wrathful Lion, and so on, all bore designations culled ingeniously from prophecy.

The great external events of history of their times were discovered in the Scriptures, predicted as signs of the last days: the Seleucid rule, the wars of the Hasmoneans, the rise of the Romans, and the conquest of Palestine by Pompey. And the internal events of sectarian life and history were rehearsed even more dramatically in the sayings of the prophets. Here we come upon one of the major difficulties in writing Essene history. Major political events and, from our point of view, minor or private events in the life of the sect are mixed in their expositions of Scripture in dizzying fashion, and, as if this were

The Judean wilderness east of Jerusalem had special religious significance by the time of the early prophets. Initially it was a place of spiritual retreat and purification. In later prophecies it was the place that would become a new Garden of Eden in the eschatological age to come.

not bad enough, the whole is veiled in the esoteric language of apocalyptic.

In sum, the Essenes of Qumran were a community formed and guided by Zadokite priests. In the latter half of the second century B.C.E., having lost hope of regaining authority in Jerusalem and under persecution by a new house of reigning priests, they fled to the desert and, finding new hope in apocalyptic dreams, readied themselves for the imminent judgment when their enemies would be vanquished and they, God's elect, would be given final victory in accordance with the prophets' predictions.

It is not difficult to identify the priestly conflict out of which the Essene party emerged. In the days of Antiochus Epiphanes (175–163 B.C.E.), the orderly succession of Zadokite high priests failed. The high-priestly office became a prize dispensed by the Seleucid overlord Antiochus, to be purchased by the highest bidder. The strife between rivals for the theocratic office soon developed into civil war, and in the resulting chaos Antiochus found opportunity to carry out his fearful massacres, terminating in the desecration of the temple and the Hellenization of Jerusalem. The stage was set for the rise of the Maccabees, who led the Jews in a heroic war of independence and who, having won popularity by freeing Judah from foreign suzerains, themselves usurped the high-priestly office. In this way, the ancient Zadokite house gave way to the lusty, if illegitimate, Hasmonean dynasty. Essene origins are to be discovered precisely in the struggle between these priestly houses and their adherents.

Perhaps the historian should say no more. Historical

allusions in Essene Biblical commentaries tempt one to reconstruct the origins of the Qumran sect more precisely. We would like to know the identity of the Wicked Priest of Jerusalem, to fix more exactly the occasion for the flight and persecution of the sectarians, and, if possible, to relate the Essene sect to the other Jewish parties, especially to the Pharisees, who came into being in the same historical milieu. Perhaps it is too much to ask the identity of the Essene Teacher or of other sectarian figures who, from the standpoint of general history, played insignificant roles.

Scholarly debate on these more precise details of Essene history continues. No consensus has fully emerged. My own views underwent a major change as the archaeological and paleographical data piled up and narrowed options. Nevertheless, I think it is very likely that the Wicked Priest of Jerusalem can be identified with the high priest Simon Maccabeus, the last and perhaps the greatest of the five Maccabean brothers. In February of 134 B.C.E., Simon together with Judas (probably his eldest son) and Mattathias his youngest toured the cities of Judah, evidently reviewing fortifi-

cations that he had built or that were in the process of construction. On their tour, Simon and his sons descended to Jericho. Jericho was administered under Simon by one Ptolemy son of Abubos. Ptolemy had ambitions to rule Judea, and he organized a plot of considerable proportions.

Ptolemy's opportunity came upon the occasion of Simon's visit to Jericho. Ptolemy held a banquet for his victims in a newly completed fortress guarding Jericho. When Simon and his sons were drunk, Ptolemy's men murdered Simon and, later, his two sons. Ultimately Ptolemy's plot failed. John Hyrcanus, Simon's remaining son, who was then in Gezer, eluded assassins sent to slay him and escaped to Jerusalem in time to rally loyal Jews against the forces sent by Ptolemy to take the city. Ptolemy sent to Antiochus VII Sidetes for immediate aid. Antiochus arrived too late to assist Ptolemy, but Antiochus was successful in reducing the country and in forcing Jerusalem to surrender.

These events comport well with certain historical allusions found in so-called List of Testimonia from Cave 4 at Qumran. One of the Testimonia refers to a "Cursed One" predicted in Joshua 6:26. The passage in Joshua follows the account of the ancient destruction of Jericho and reads as follows:

WILDERNESS WANDERING

To escape persecution in Jerusalem, the Essenes fled to the desert wilderness in hopes of finding victory, as God had promised, over their enemies. These desertscapes reflect the kind of barren land the Essenes chose for their escape.

Cursed before the LORD be anyone who tries to rebuild this city—this Jericho! At the cost of his firstborn he shall lay its foundation, and at the cost of his youngest he shall set up its gates! (NRSV)

The curse was once fulfilled when in the ninth century B.C.E. Jericho was rebuilt by a certain Hiel, with the loss of his sons (see 1 Kings 16:34). The Essenes chose this particular text, once fulfilled, and reapplied it to their own time. The Testimonia, partly reconstructed, reads in part as follows:

And behold, a cursed man, a man of Belial, shall come to power to be a trapper's snare and ruin to all his neighbors, and he shall come to power and [his sons] … [with him], the two of them becoming violent instruments, and they shall rebuild again the [city … and shall set] up a wall and towers for it, to make a stronghold of wickedness [in the land and a great evil] in Israel and horrors in Ephraim and in Judah. … [and they shall commit sacrilege in the land, and great abuse among the children of [Jacob and blo]od [shall be poured out] like water on the battlement of the daughter of Zion and in the district of Jerusalem.

If we follow the pattern of close apocalyptic exegesis that normally obtains in sectarian exposition of Scripture, we must look for an event connected with the fortification of Jericho by a major enemy of the sect when the dreadful curse of Joshua repeated itself. And properly, we must look for a high priest of Jerusalem who associated his sons with him in his rule.

The events concerning the murder of Simon and his two sons in Jericho when they came to inspect the new fortifications at Jericho, as well as the bloody aftermath of their triple assassination, seem to explain adequately the resurrection of the old curse on Jericho by the Essenes. Most of the elements of the prophecy fit strikingly: the association of the cursed man with two sons in the fortification overlooking Jericho; their death at the hands of Ptolemy's henchmen as evidence of the effectiveness of the curse; and the subsequent devastation and bloodshed in Judah and Jerusalem. I find it difficult not to conclude that Simon is established as the Cursed Man of the Testimonia.

Is this "Cursed Man" identical with the Wicked Priest? The other Testimonia relate to the messianic prophet, priest, and king, as well as to the priestly forerunner of the new age who founded the sect. The juxtaposition of the Cursed Man with the other central figures of the sect strongly suggests that the Cursed Man is in fact the Wicked Priest.

Jonathan (162–142 B.C.E.), the second of the Maccabean brothers, was the first to usurp the high-priestly office, and some have suggested that he should

An Organized Complex

This complex of rooms is located at the center of the Qumran building complex, and the activities carried out here may have been at the center of Qumran communal life: the study and copying of Biblical texts and prophecies. The long room in the center (A) was identified as the "scriptorium," where new copies of sacred writings were made by scribes. The first room on the right (B) may have been a study hall for reading and teaching from texts. A smaller room (C) off the study hall might have been the library or, perhaps, a storage room for the sacred scrolls.

be identified with the Wicked Priest. Several factors, however, make this unlikely. Jonathan's position was tenuous throughout his term. Jewish independence was not to be fully won until the reign of Simon. To the end of his days Jonathan struggled to maintain himself against foreign foes. It seems unlikely that he was secure enough to turn on fellow Jews and persecute the

Zadokites (Essenes); moreover, in view of the de facto nature of his rule and the uncertainty of the times, the Zadokite priests would not have abandoned hope and fled Jerusalem upon the occasion of Jonathan's donning of the high-priestly robes. On the contrary, we should expect that move only to initiate hostilities between the orthodox and the Maccabean nationalists.

S imon, Jonathan's successor, brought to fulfillment his brothers' national dreams. In the second year of his rule he succeeded in driving out the Syrian garrison from the citadel in Jerusalem. Judea only then became fully free of the Seleucid yoke. Simon ruled in peace and was at liberty to consolidate his realm. In 140 B.C.E., the third year of his reign, a great assembly was held "of the priests and people and heads of the nation and the elders of the country." The work of the assembly and the significance of its decree for the history of the high priesthood cannot be overestimated. The decree of the assembly was engraved in bronze and set up on stelae on Mount Zion. Simon was made high priest *de jure,* and the high priesthood was given to Simon's house forever, "until a faithful prophet should arise" (1 Maccabees 14:30–39). The claim is here made to a legal transference of the high priesthood from the Zadokite dynasty (appointed by David!) to the Hasmonean dynasty. The illegitimacy of Simon's house is admitted tacitly in the phrase "until a faithful prophet arise," that is, until a final arbiter between the rival houses appears in the age to come. Further, the decree warned against any opposition to Simon by layman or priest, prohibited private assembly, and threatened punishment to anyone who acted contrary to the stipulations of the decree.

I n this decree we can clearly discern the new high priest's determination to stamp out opposition, to persecute those who refused to recognize the full legitimacy of his office. This program seems to give the appropriate occasion for the crystallization of the Essene sect, its persecution and the persecution of the Righteous Teacher, and the exile in the wilderness of Judah. Simon had the leisure, power, popularity, and inclination to root out Jewish opposition to the ascendancy of his party and his house. Certain texts, especially the Testimonia, support our identification of the Wicked Priest with Simon. Finally, the archaeological evidence for the dating of the foundation of the community fits more easily with a date in Simon's reign than with a date in Jonathan's reign.

I have not dealt, of course, with a large number of texts relating to the Wicked Priest and his relations with the Righteous Teacher and the exiled community. Most fit equally well with Jonathan or Simon, or indeed with a number of other priests. In this era one cannot complain of a shortage of wicked priests. One final text, however, deserves mention. In a passage of the Commentary on Habakkuk, the expositor comments, "This means the priest whose dishonor was greater than his honor. For he … walked in the ways of drunkenness in order to quench his thirst. But the cup of God's wrath will swallow him up…!" The high priest caroused once too often. In Jericho, at the hands of Ptolemy, the cup of pleasure turned into the cup of wrath and swallowed Simon. So I would interpret the text.

I have been able to fix the general framework of the Essene community's life in the desert. Perhaps I have succeeded also in identifying the villain of the esoteric commentaries. No doubt, I have also illustrated the complexities and frustrations that face the student of the Essene library from Qumran.

GOOD OVER EVIL

Many of the Dead Sea Scrolls pit two unnamed figures against each other: the Righteous Teacher and the Wicked Priest (also known as the Lion of Wrath, the Liar, the Spreader of Lies, and the Man of Scoffing). The Qumran commentary on Habakkuk 2:15 relates this prophecy to the deadly conflict between these two archenemies. In the end, the commentary promises that God will pour out his wrath on the Wicked Priest and utterly destroy him.

NOTES

1. As claimed by G. R. Driver, for example, in his erratic and arbitrary study, *The Judaean Scrolls* (Oxford: Blackwell, 1965).

2. See W. F. Albright, "A Biblical Fragment from the Maccabean Age: The Nash Papyrus," *Journal of Biblical Literature* 56 (1937):145–76.

3. See F. M. Cross, "The Development of Jewish Scripts," in G. Ernest Wright, ed., *The Bible and the Ancient Near East,* 133–202.

UNCOVERING BURIED TREASURE

Materials in Caves 4 and 5 were not simply lying on the surface. They were buried under more than six feet of bat dung and wind-blown dust that had accumulated over the centuries.

PUBLISHING THE SCROLLS

Reflections on 30 Years of Involvement with the Scrolls

By Emanuel Tov

The past fifteen years have witnessed a virtual "explosion" in the publication of ancient texts from Qumran and the surrounding area. Thanks primarily to the significant involvement of the Israel Antiquities Authority, the reorganization of the publication team, financial support received from several organizations, and computerized publication procedures, critical editions of all the Dead Sea Scrolls and numerous other texts from sites nearby (more than 1,500 texts in all) are now available to scholars and the general public alike. This article, which draws on my experience as editor-in-chief of the Discoveries in the Judaean Desert series, discusses the general contents of the Dead Sea Scrolls, especially those of the Hebrew Bible, describes what was involved in working with them, and narrates some of the complications that we faced in preparing them for publication.

The Scrolls from Qumran and Nearby

The various texts discovered in the caves at Qumran are generally divided into four discrete categories.

1. Biblical texts. More than two hundred Biblical scrolls (texts of Hebrew Scripture) were found in the caves at Qumran and other sites in the Judean Desert. There is only one scroll, however, of a complete book, in this case a long one: the Isaiah text from Cave 1, named 1QIsa^a. Most of the fragmentary texts are small, containing no more than one-tenth of a Biblical book. Fragments have been found of all the Biblical books except Esther and Nehemiah. (Note that Ezra-Nehemiah form one book in the Hebrew Bible, and a fragment of Ezra was found at Qumran.)

The oldest Biblical manuscripts known before 1947 dated from a very late period in the transmission of the Biblical text—from the Middle Ages. The Qumran texts and fragments of the Hebrew Bible go back to a time as early as the third century B.C.E., bringing our knowledge about the text of the Bible back more than one thousand years, significantly closer to the time of composition of the books themselves.

2. Sectarian texts. The inhabitants of Qumran, usually identified as the Essenes (see the previous chapter by Frank Moore Cross), produced a vast body of

GENESIS RETOLD FROM OLD

The Genesis Apocryphon retells the stories of Noah and Abraham but embellishes the traditional accounts found in the book of Genesis. The text was written in Aramaic, and only one copy has been found. Note the deteriorated condition of the scroll, which makes it difficult to unroll and reconstruct the remaining fragmentary portions of text. Special photographic techniques have been helpful in reconstructing text that cannot be read with the naked eye.

their own literature, which we now call "sectarian" due to the nature of their community. These compositions reflect the views of the Qumranites themselves about what was happening in the world around them, about what life in the hereafter would be like, and about how they could prove to themselves and others that the Hebrew Bible, when explained "correctly," already reflected the sectarians' views.

3. Other Jewish compositions from the Second Temple period. These compositions were written by various Jewish groups outside of Qumran. In some cases, however, the origin of the text cannot be determined with certainty. Some of these compositions were known previously from the Greek translation of the Hebrew Bible, called the Septuagint (abbreviated LXX). These ancient compositions included in the LXX were eventually excluded from the canon of the Hebrew Bible. Traditionally these books have been called apocryphal or deuterocanonical works. Other extra-Biblical works not included in the canon of the LXX have traditionally been labeled pseudepigraphal, and examples of these—*Enoch* is the best known—were also found at Qumran. Still other books in this category are previously unknown Jewish works.

4. Nonliterary texts. Small fragments of some thirty nonliterary works, mainly lists and contracts, were also found at Qumran, and many additional such texts were found at other sites (see below).

n addition to the Qumran caves where inscriptional materials were discovered between 1947 and 1962—the Dead Sea Scrolls, *in stricto sensu*—other texts were discovered by Bedouin and archaeologists at a number of other sites, from the Wadi ed-Daliyeh north of Jericho to Masada in the south (see map of sites). For example, the texts from Wadi ed-Daliyeh consist of a large group of legal and administrative texts written in Aramaic on papyrus and sealed with clay bullae, dating from 375 to 335 B.C.E.[1]

Various texts reportedly from Nahal Se'elim, Nahal Hever, Murabba'at, and Masada include fragments of Hebrew, Aramaic, and Greek Biblical and legal documents, including deeds, contracts, and divorce decrees, several hundred documents in all. Five Nabatean contracts have also been found. The stars of the collection are several letters in Aramaic from Murabba'at written to Bar-Kokhba, the leader of the Second Jewish Revolt against Rome (132–135 C.E.).

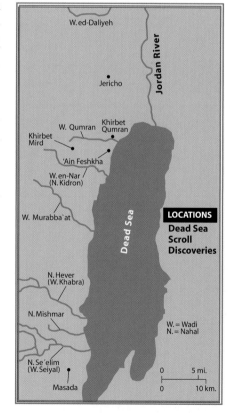

LOCATIONS

Dead Sea Scroll Discoveries

W. = Wadi
N. = Nahal

0   5 mi.
0   10 km.

Publication Challenges and Solutions

The tens of thousands of fragments of written material from the Judean Desert needed to be deciphered, sorted, catalogued, photographed, commented upon, and, in the case of non-Biblical scrolls, translated. This enormous task was initially entrusted to a team of scholars that, in hindsight, was much too small. This miscalculation resulted in an overlong (and often critized) delay in publication. One should not forget, however, that the original team consisted of truly great scholars who devoted all their time to producing thorough and original work, as seen in the early volumes of the Discoveries in the Judaean Desert series (DJD), the official publication of the Dead Sea Scrolls by Clarendon Press at Oxford University, as well as in dozens of preliminary publications.

Nevertheless, to obtain a reasonable pace of publication, significant reorganization had to be undertaken. The previous editor-in-chief, John Strugnell, set the ball rolling by adding nearly twenty scholars to the team. Working in close collaboration with the Advisory Committee of the Israel Antiquities Authority (IAA), activated by the strong leadership of its director, General Amir Drori, I enlarged the editorial team by fifty-three scholars. The invitation to join the team was issued by the Advisory Committee of the IAA upon suggestions made by the editor-in-chief. In the course of these activities I was supported by Professor Eugene Ulrich of the University of Notre Dame and Monsieur L'Abbé Emile Puech of the École Biblique of Jerusalem.

NUMBER OF SCROLLS SCHOLARS PER COUNTRY (1991–PRESENT)

United States	25
Israel	17
Netherlands	3
England	2
France	2
Germany	2
Canada	1
Norway	1
Spain	1

DEAD SEA SCROLLS STATS

➤ **Number of scrolls: about 930**

➤ **Number of intact scrolls: about 12 (depending on what one considers intact)**

➤ **Number of fragmentary scrolls: about 920**

➤ **Date first scrolls found: 1947 or 1948**

➤ **Date last scroll found: 1962 (2003)**

➤ **Editors-in-Chief:**

Roland de Vaux, 1952–1975, 5 vols.

Pierre Benoit, 1975–1984, 2 vols.

John Strugnell, 1984–1990, 1 vol.

Emanuel Tov, 1990–present, 30 vols.

➤ **Number of scholars on original scroll publication team: 8**

➤ **Number of Jews on original scroll publication team: 0**

➤ **Number of scholars added to publication team by Benoit: 18**

➤ **Number of scholars added to publication team by Strugnell: 18**

➤ **Number of scholars added to publication team by Tov: 53**

➤ **Total scholars who edited scrolls: 98**

➤ **Total number of pages in volumes published in the DJD series: 11,984**

➤ **Total number of plates of photographs in volumes published in the DJD series: 1,339**

Half of the final team assigned to edit and publish the scrolls were senior scholars; half, junior scholars specializing in texts from the Judean Desert. Proven expertise in publishing the difficult texts from Qumran remained the main criterion for inclusion in this international enterprise. While Jews had been excluded in the past, the team eventually included Catholic, Protestant, and Jewish scholars.

Decipherment was the major task facing the editors of the scrolls. Of necessity, all the editors had to become experts in reading these sometimes hardly legible texts. Some texts, of course, are more difficult than others. For example, in some fragments the iron-based ink has corroded and eaten through the leather, creating the impression of a negative. At times this process led to the disintegration of the leather itself.

Most of the Qumran documents are written in Hebrew; the second largest group is in Aramaic. A few are in Greek, and Nabatean documents have also been found at some sites.

Two forms of Semitic script are used in the Qumran texts: the Aramaic or "square" script that the Jews brought back with them from the Babylonian exile; and the so called paleo-Hebrew script, continuing the "early" Hebrew script, in which Hebrew documents had been written before the adoption of the square Aramaic script.

In addition, Qumran also presented scholars with two previously unknown scripts. A member of the initial team, J. T. Milik, at first identified them as one and dubbed them the "Cryptic Script." They are now recognized as two scripts: Cryptic A and Cryptic B. The language of documents written in both scripts is Hebrew.

One of the challenges that we faced was in providing standard, accurate, and informative designations for the texts. To that end, I created and published a list of then-unpublished texts from Qumran Caves 4 and 11.[2] This list provided the following information: the sequential number in the list of the manuscripts of the Qumran inventory, such as 4Q201 (that is, item 201 among the fragments from Q[umran] Cave 4); the name of the composition, such as En[a] (this stands for *Enoch,* copy a); previous sigla; the name(s) of the editor(s) of the text; references to preliminary publications of the text(s); and notes on the material on which the text is written (papyrus or leather), the language, and the script. In compiling this list I was much helped by the individual editors, who took great care in providing the most up-to-date information available.

Obviously, these bare data gave only minimal information about the texts. For those of us on the editorial team, however, the list told a story of its own, and many of its details revealed aspects of the complicated and ever-changing nature of our enterprise.

Consider, for example, the number of compositions on the list. How does one distinguish between two different compositions if all one has are two tiny fragments? Script (handwriting)

TOOLS OF ANCIENT SCRIBES

Excavators discovered that the rubble filling this long, rectangular room, presumably used for writing Biblical texts (a scriptorium), contained the remains of a writing table, bench, and inkwells.

One of these Qumran inkwells was found near the scriptorium, and two were found in the room. The middle inkwell is made of bronze, the other two of pottery.

is the main criterion for distinguishing between compositions. For example, what in the past was called 4QJer^b (Jeremiah, text b, from Cave 4), consisting of three different fragments, is now assigned to three different scrolls (named 4QJer^b, 4QJer^d, and 4QJer^e) due to differences in their scripts, scribal features, and content. Obviously, decisions are often very difficult. For example, if a scribe penned several manuscripts of similar or identical content on similar leather, fragments now assigned to a single inventory number may in fact represent the remains of two or more different compositions. Because of these difficulties, the exact number of compositions represented in/among the scroll fragments will never be known.

Yet another aspect illustrating the complicated nature of the editorial process is reflected in the occasional change of the names of compositions. These names are part of the designations of individual compositions. Editors changed the name of a composition for a number of reasons.

1. At times, *specific* names of Qumran texts were replaced by more general ones; for example, various documents named Mishmarot, "priestly courses" (a specific name), are now called Calendrical Documents (a more general name, given because not all fragments are concerned with the courses of the priests).

2. Many of the once general names were made more specific. A text once called "poetic fragment" (4Q448) has been renamed and subsequently published as "Apocryphal Psalm and Prayer."

3. Names were changed due to better understanding of the major figures or topics featured in a specific composition. Two of the fragments of 4QpsEzek (pseudo-Ezekiel) have become 4QApocrJer (Apocryphal Jeremiah, 4Q385a, 387).

4. At the same time, several documents retain at this stage such general names as "sapiential text," "prayer," "work containing prayers," "liturgy," and "apocryphon."

SONGS AND PSALMS

One of the first seven scrolls found in Qumran Cave 1 was a collection of "Thanksgiving Psalms." This scroll is referred to as Hodayot (thanks) because many of the roughly 25 hymns it contains begin with *'odekah 'adonay* (I thank you, O Lord).

These hymns, or prayers, are similar in style to the Biblical psalms. They often quote directly or paraphrase language in the canonical psalms and in the "Servant Song" sections in Isaiah. Fragmentary copies of this scroll were also found in Cave 4.

The benefits of the computer age were also brought to bear upon the enormous task of organizing and cataloguing the thousands of Dead Sea Scrolls fragments. For example, an electronic database of the inventory I prepared with the help of Stephen Pfann helped me over the course of the past fifteen years to manage the enormous amount of data pertaining to all the individual fragments, their photographs, and their publication. It is not difficult to imagine how hard it is to work with this material without the use of computers in light of the frequent changes in designations and the arrangement of fragments and the complicated photographic recording of the fragments. With regard to the latter, numerous photographs of the fragments were taken in the 1950s and early 1960s, as the fragments were sorted and arranged according to compositions and subsequently rearranged according to a renewed understanding of those compositions. This process was recorded at various stages by photographs taken time and time again (mainly on infrared film) by the photographer of the Palestine Archaeological Museum (PAM). Later photographs were taken by the Israel Antiquities Authority. These series of photographs thus represent "generations" in the compilation and arrangement of the fragments of each manuscript.

The database was organized in such a way that information of different types was contained in various fields in the computer file. This allowed us to search for certain types of information in one field only or in all of them. One could sort according to special features, such as collecting all the documents written in either the paleo-Hebrew script, Cryptic A, or Greek. At the same time, information regarding inventory numbers, photographic numbers, editors, the size of documents, and the number of fragments was also at hand. All this information in a "final" form has now been made available in the introductory volume to the DJD series, which in good scholarly fashion has been published as the almost last volume (vol. 39, 2002).

Noteworthy Extra-Biblical Texts

Prior to their publication over the past decades, a great deal of speculation centered on what some of the

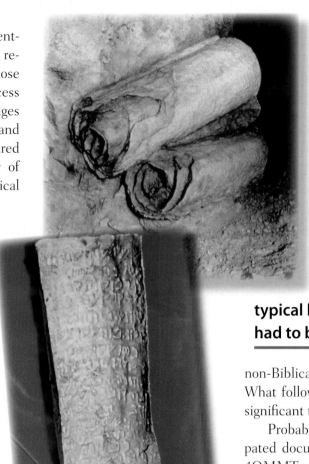

The copper rolls were not scrolls at all, in the traditional sense. They were sheets of copper joined by rivets that could more properly be called *plaques*.

A startling discovery in 1952 was this scroll made of copper, found in two pieces on a natural rock ledge inside Cave 3. The green patina covering the surface is evidence of oxidation, which left the copper too fragile and brittle to be unrolled like a typical leather scroll. This scroll had to be sawn apart.

non-Biblical Dead Sea Scrolls contained. What follows are examples of especially significant texts within this corpus.

Probably the most eagerly anticipated document was the text known as 4QMMT or 4QMiqsat Ma'ase Ha-Torah ("Some of the Works of the Law," also known as "Halakhic Letter"). Preserved in six different manuscripts (4Q394–399), MMT probably contains a letter by the leader of the Dead Sea Scroll community to an outside source and describes in great detail the differences in legal views between the sect and the outsiders. The views of the community are, as reflected here, so close to the Sadducees that it is now believed by many scholars that the Dead Sea Scroll community was an off-shoot of the Sadducees.

Another eagerly awaited publication was the pseudepigraphic book of *Jubilees* (4Q216–227), known previously only from Latin and Ethiopic translations made from a no-longer-extant Greek translation of a Semitic text. Fragments of this Semitic text were found at Qumran in both Aramaic and Hebrew versions. *Jubilees* provides a rewritten text of the story of Genesis, with the years subdivided into groups of fifty years. Each fiftieth year was a Jubilee year.[3]

Several sectarian documents in poetry and prose give us further details of the intellectual and devotional world of the Qumran sect. Thus several texts from Cave 4 (4Q260–4Q264) present many segments of the so-called Rule of the Community already known from its more complete copy from Cave 1 (also known as the Manual of Discipline).

A document with the siglum 4Q448 contains part of an apocryphal psalm, hitherto known only in Syriac (as Psalm 154), as well as a prayer for the well-being of King Jonathan. This is one of the few Qumran documents that contains the name of a historical figure. According to Esti and Hanan Eshel and Ada Yardeni, the text refers to the Jewish monarch Alexander Jannaeus, who reigned from 103 to 76 B.C.E.

Previously unknown lists of priestly courses, mishmarot (4Q320-330), now known as Calendrical Documents, mention the priestly families who were to serve on certain days in the temple. These manuscripts provide evidence of the sect's calendar, which differed from that of other segments of the population in Israel at the time.

The book of Tobit (4Q196–199), one of the Apocrypha, hitherto known only in Greek translation, was found in different Aramaic and Hebrew manuscripts in Qumran.

The so-called Damascus Covenant, a sectarian document linked to the Qumran community describing its history and laws, was previously known only from a copy found in the Cairo Genizah at the end of the last century. Fragments from at least eight manuscripts of that composition were found in Cave 4, reinforcing the sectarian background of the composition.

The Biblical Manuscripts from Qumran

Because my special interest is the Biblical manuscripts, I will discuss them at somewhat greater length. Fragments of more than 200 Biblical scrolls were found in the eleven Qumran caves, most of them small. Isaiah is the exception, since we have the full text of that book in the great Isaiah Scroll from Cave 1.

The script of the Biblical texts serves as the main criterion for distinguishing between the supposedly different copies even when only tiny fragments have been preserved. But one must be cautious in making an estimate of the number of the scrolls on the basis of small fragments. Two scribes could have written a single scroll, or the same scribe could have written more than one scroll.

Three of the scrolls—apparently originally scrolls of the whole Torah—contain two consecutive books.

Some Biblical books were especially popular among the Qumranites. There were thirty-six copies of the book of Psalms found at Qumran, thirty copies of Deuteronomy (including two in paleo-Hebrew script), between twenty and twenty-four copies of Isaiah, as many as twenty copies of Genesis (three in paleo-

Surgical Skills a Must

Damaged fragments of the Temple Scroll are pieced together with surgical precision by Joseph "Dodo" Shenhav and Ruth Yekutieli of the Israel Museum. These fragments were part of a "wad," a few pieces that had been separated recently from the main scroll.

Hebrew script), and seventeen copies of Exodus (two in paleo-Hebrew script).

The Biblical manuscripts can be divided into five different groups, mostly on the basis of the similar content of each textual grouping.

Some texts are what we call proto-Masoretic. The Masoretic Text is the so-called *textus receptus* ("received text") among Jews. The fully developed Masoretic Text, or MT, as it is often called, was standardized in about the tenth century with its vocalization, accentuation, and Masoretic apparatus of notes and comments. The proto-Masoretic texts from Qumran are examples of the Hebrew texts that lie behind the MT. The special textual characteristic of these proto-Masoretic texts from Qumran is their agreement with the medieval MT. The proto-Masoretic texts constitute about 50 percent of the Qumran Biblical texts. The great preponderance of these texts at Qumran shows that in the last centuries before the turn of the era and the first century C.E. the official text of the temple circles was diffused widely in Israel.

Some texts are pre-Samaritan texts; that is, these Qumran texts are very close to the Samaritan Pentateuch. It appears that one of them formed the basis of the Samaritan text.

The third group of Biblical texts is close to the presumed Hebrew source of the Septuagint (LXX). Although no text has been found in Qumran that is identical or even almost identical with the presumed Hebrew source of the LXX, a few texts are very close to it.

Together the pre-Samaritan texts and the texts close to the presumed Hebrew source of the LXX constitute only about 10 percent of the Qumran Biblical texts.

The fourth group of Qumran Biblical texts are so-called nonaligned texts (average of 40 percent). Many texts are not exclusively close to any one of the textual groups mentioned above. These texts agree, sometimes significantly, with the MT against the other texts, or they agree with the Samaritan Pentateuch and/or the LXX against the other texts, but the nonaligned texts also disagree with the other texts to the same extent. Furthermore, they contain readings not known from the other texts, so that they are not exclusively close to one of the

Why Are the Scrolls Important? Excerpt from an Interview with Emanuel Tov

by Hershel Shanks

HS: I think that everybody from plumbers and taxicab drivers to professors has heard of the Dead Sea Scrolls, but when you get to the next question and ask, "What do they say?" you almost always get the answer, "I don't know." What is the most important thing we learn from the scrolls?

ET: One thing we learned from the scrolls is, they don't make a difference for Judaism or Christianity. We are all asked the same question: Do they make a difference for our Christian or Jewish religion? Well, they don't. However, the Dead Sea Scrolls *are* important for the scholarly investigation of ancient Israel; they include ancient Israelite literature from the Bible to the second century C.E. Scholarship on this period is not imaginable any more without looking into the Dead Sea Scrolls. Textual criticism of the Hebrew Scriptures, my own area of expertise, is not imaginable without the Dead Sea Scrolls.

other textual groups. This characterization is important when one tries to determine the full range of texts current in the Second Temple period.

Finally, many Qumran Biblical texts are what we call texts written in the "Qumran practice." These texts are written in the Qumran system of orthography (spelling), morphology (linguistic features), and scribal practice and reflect a free approach to the Biblical text, with adaptations of unusual forms to the context, frequent errors, numerous corrections, and, sometimes, negligent script. These texts were probably written by one scribal school, possibly in Qumran. The large Isaiah Scroll from Cave 1, 1QIsaᵃ, is a good example of such a text.

The coexistence of all these different categories of texts in the Qumran caves is in itself noteworthy. The fact that all these different texts were found in the same Qumran caves probably reflects a certain textual reality in the period between the third century B.C.E. and the first century C.E. This situation may be described as textual plurality and variety reflected in the Biblical Qumran texts.

A few additional Biblical manuscripts are of special importance. Some small fragments of Jeremiah (4Q71–71a, 4QJerᵇ and 4QJerᵈ) contain a Hebrew text very similar to the LXX. Both the Qumran fragments and the Greek translation differ in major details from the MT. This text is much shorter, by one-sixth, and the sequence of the verses and chapters sometimes differs. These deviating texts reflect a different *content* edition of the book of Jeremiah, not just a different text.

Finally, an important text of Samuel (4Q51, 4QSamᵃ) is in many details superior to the traditional Hebrew text, which is often at fault.

A Final Word

Much has changed in the years since I became editor-in-chief of the Scrolls publication team. Thanks to the efforts of the editors, all of the scrolls that have been found are now in the public domain in scholarly editions. In addition, interested scholars may freely access photographs of those texts needed for research or simply because of a desire to see them. Further, all the texts, translations, and images of the scrolls can now be accessed conveniently on CD.[4] It is a good time for the scrolls. It is a good time for scholars.

Still, important work remains to be done, especially in interpreting the scrolls. Above all, Qumran scholarship needs to be integrated into the scholarship of other disciplines. People who study Jewish law should study not only the rabbinic texts but also the Qumran documents. Likewise, Biblical scholars need to incorporate evidence from the Dead Sea Scrolls into their studies, whether their focus is on textual criticism, early prayer, apocalyptic literature, and so forth. While we wait for the completion of the printed concordance of the Scrolls and for three volumes of improved editions of texts published earlier, we consider ourselves lucky to have all this rich material available. Now that all the scrolls have been made available, it is indeed the dawn of an exciting new era in the world of Dead Sea Scrolls research.

NOTES

1. Frank Moore Cross, "The Historical Importance of the Samaria Papyri," *Biblical Archaeology Review* 4/1 (March 1978): 25–27.

2. Emanuel Tov, "The Unpublished Qumran Texts from Caves 4 and 11," *Journal of Jewish Studies* 43 (1992): 101–36. A revised version of that list appeared in *Biblical Archaeologist* 55/2 (June 1992): 94–104.

3. See James C. VanderKam, "Jubilees: How It Rewrote the Bible," *Bible Review* 8/6 (December 1992): 32–39, 60.

4. *The Dead Sea Scrolls Electronic Library* (Brigham Young University; rev. ed., 2006), part of the *Dead Sea Scrolls Electronic Reference Library* (ed. Emanuel Tov; Leiden: Brill, 2006).

Although scholars have long known that the precise limits of the Hebrew Bible remained fluid for centuries, the Dead Sea Scrolls reveal that even the text of key portions of the Bible was subject to change when the Scrolls were written.

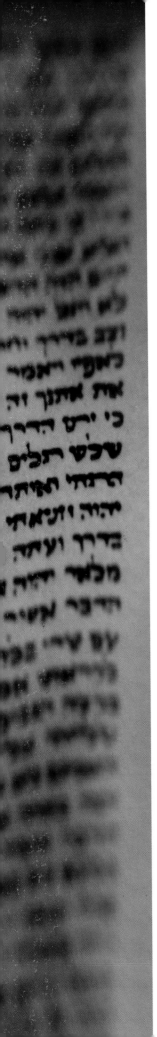

THE FLUID BIBLE

The Blurry Line Between Biblical and Nonbiblical Texts

By Sidnie White Crawford

When the Dead Sea Scrolls were written some two thousand years ago, no canonical Bible existed. That is, in the two or three centuries before the Roman destruction of the Jerusalem temple in 70 C.E., there was no single list of sacred books that was considered authoritative. At the same time, there was no clear border between biblical books and nonbiblical books. Rather, different groups of Jews considered different books authoritative, even though all Jews accepted the Torah, or Pentateuch—that is, the books of Genesis, Exodus, Leviticus, Numbers and Deuteronomy. The Torah was, after all, the source of the law, which provided the underpinning of Jewish religious practice and daily life.

Although scholars have long recognized this fluidity for a good portion of the Hebrew Bible, the Dead Sea Scrolls reveal another surprising fact: even in the case of the Torah, there was no fixed text either of the Torah as a whole or of any of the individual books. Rather, among the scrolls we find a whole group of texts that are related to, but different from, the present-day books of the canonical Torah.

Some of the texts are simply copies of biblical books with variants, the result of centuries of hand-copying (scribal error or manipulation) and textual growth. These documents provide critical new material to the text critic who attempts to recover the best text of a biblical book, using all the copies available.

Some of these texts, however, differ markedly—at times startlingly—from the standard authoritative Jewish version of the Bible, known as the Masoretic Text (MT for short). Nor do they resemble the two other major biblical textual traditions, the Septuagint (or LXX for short) and the Samaritan Pentateuch.

The Septuagint is a Greek translation made for the Jews of Alexandria, Egypt, the first five books of which were translated in the third century B.C.E. from a Hebrew text that differs somewhat from MT. (According to legend, the name Septuagint, which comes from the Latin term for "seventy," refers to the seventy-two Jewish translators brought to Egypt by Ptolemy Philadelphus [285–246 B.C.E.] to translate the Torah.) I will have more to say about the Samaritan Pentateuch later. Suffice it to say for now that MT is the authoritative text for Jews and Protestants; LXX, for the Orthodox churches; and the Samaritan Pentateuch, for the small group of Samaritans who still live in Nablus and a few places in Israel. What is important to note for our purposes is that each of these traditions is represented in various fragmentary manuscripts of the Pentateuch found among the Dead Sea Scrolls.

However, some of the seemingly biblical manuscripts from Qumran differ considerably from *all* of these traditions. The question I would raise is, In ancient times, how far could these texts deviate and still be considered biblical? Or authoritative? Scholars themselves are somewhat unsure, calling them "parabiblical" or "quasibiblical." Those terms, however, describe the texts only from our viewpoint. To us, they are not canonical and therefore cannot be biblical. But to the people who copied and read them two thousand years ago, they may have been just as authoritative as the texts we consider biblical today.

Let's look at a few of these "parabiblical" texts. Our first example is a Dead Sea Scroll called 4QDeuteronomy^n, which was copied in the late first century B.C.E. and which contains a text of the Ten Commandments.[1] (The "4Q" that appears so often in Dead Sea Scroll designations stands for Qumran Cave 4, where more than five hundred different manuscripts, all fragmentary, were found.) The Ten Commandments appear in two places in our canonical Torah—in Exodus 20 and in Deuteronomy 5—but the two versions are not exactly the same. The fourth commandment in Exodus (20:8–11) bids the Israelites to "remember" the Sabbath day. In Deuteronomy (5:12–15), however, the Israelites are commanded to "observe" the Sabbath day. And that's not all: *the rationales differ in Exodus and Deuteronomy.* In Exodus, the Israelites must remember the Sabbath because the Lord rested on the seventh day after creating the universe in six days. In Deuteronomy, the reason given is that they were slaves in Egypt.

The two different versions were already well established by the time the Dead Sea Scrolls were copied. How do we know this? Because both are referred to in 4QDeuteronomy^n. As shown in the chart on page 55, 4QDeuteronomy^n presents yet another version of this commandment. Here the scribe begins with the Deuteronomy version ("Observe the Sabbath day") and gives Deuteronomy's reasoning: "And remember that you were a servant in the land of Egypt. ... therefore the LORD your God has commanded

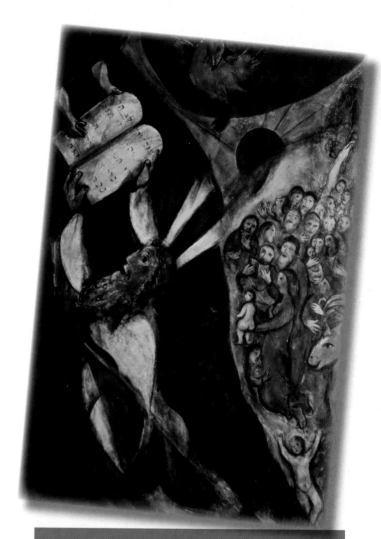

Ten Commandments Times Two

Heavenly hands pass Moses the Decalogue, in Marc Chagall's "Moses Receives the Tablets of the Law" (1950–1952). The Ten Commandments appear in two different versions in the Hebrew Bible (Exodus 20 and Deuteronomy 5). A first-century B.C.E. Dead Sea Scroll (4QDeuteronomy^n) harmonizes both into one long Sabbath commandment—but not at the expense of the text's authority. To the contrary, as author Sidnie White Crawford demonstrates, variants in a sacred text may have enhanced, rather than reduced, its sacred status.

you to observe the Sabbath day to sanctify it." But the text doesn't stop there. Rather, it picks up with the justification given in Exodus: "For six days the Lord made the heavens and the earth, the sea ... and he rested on the seventh day; therefore, the LORD blessed the Sab-

ONE COMMANDMENT, THREE VERSIONS

Why should the Israelites observe the Sabbath day? The answer in the Hebrew Bible is not so straightforward. According to the book of Exodus (quoted in italic type in the left column), it's because after six days of creation, God rested on the seventh day. But Deuteronomy (center, underlined) offers a somewhat different explanation: the Israelites should rest because they were once slaves in Egypt. Both these documents must have been in circulation at the time the Dead Sea Scrolls were composed, since an enterprising scribe tried to straighten out the confusion in a manuscript known today as 4QDeuteronomy^n, which combines the message of both Exodus (in italics) and Deuteronomy (underlined), as shown in the right column.

Exodus (20:8–11)	Deuteronomy (5:12–15)	4QDeuteronomy^n
Remember the Sabbath day, and keep it holy.	Observe the Sabbath day and keep it holy, as the LORD your God commanded you.	Observe the Sabbath day, to sanctify it, *as the LORD your God has commanded you.*
Six days you shall labor and do all your work. But the seventh day is a Sabbath to the LORD your God; you shall not do any work— you, your son or your daughter, your male or female slave,	Six days you shall labor and do all your work. But the seventh day is a Sabbath to the LORD your God; you shall not do any work— you, or your son or your daughter, or your male or female slave, or your ox or your donkey, or any of your livestock,	*Six days you shall labor and do all your work, but on the seventh day is a Sabbath to the LORD your God; you shall not do in it any work, you, your son, your daughter, your male servant or your female servant, your ox or your ass*
your livestock, or the alien resident in your towns.	or the resident alien in your towns, so that your male and female slave may rest as well as you. Remember that you were a slave in the land of Egypt, and the LORD your God brought you out from there with a mighty hand and an outstretched arm; therefore the Lord your God command-ed you to keep the Sabbath day.	or your beast, *your sojourner who is in your gates;* in order that your male servant and your female servant might rest like you. And remember that you were a servant in the land of Egypt, and the LORD your God brought you forth from there with a mighty hand and an outstretched arm; therefore the LORD your God has com-manded you to observe the Sabbath day to sanctify it.
For in six days the LORD made heaven and earth, the sea, and all that is in them, but rested the seventh day; therefore the LORD blessed the Sabbath day and consecrated it.		*For six days the LORD made the heavens and the earth, the sea and all which is in them, and he rested on the seventh day; therefore the LORD blessed the Sabbath day to sanctify it.*

bath day to sanctify it." The scribe has smoothed out, or harmonized, the two texts by combining both justifications into one (very long!) Sabbath commandment.[2]

What did first-century readers think when encountering this text? We can only speculate, but probably they would have recognized it as a harmonization of the other two existing versions. After all, at the time there probably were other manuscripts of Exodus and Deuteronomy that contained the Ten Commandments in the versions with which we are familiar today.[3] So a careful reader would have recognized that a change had been made. But would that have made any difference to the authority of the text? Probably not. This seems to be a major difference between Second Temple period Jews (living before the Roman destruction of 70 C.E.) and the modern Jewish or Christian reader.

For Second Temple period Jews, the authority of these sacred books lay in each book's general message rather than in its precise words or in their order.[4] The words of the biblical text could be manipulated—moved around, updated, added to—without detracting from the authoritative status of the book. This may not have been true for all Jews in the Second Temple period, but it certainly seems to have been true for the Jews of Palestine.

Thus, in 4QDeuteronomy[n] the important point is the command to observe the Sabbath, which is unchanging; importing text from Exodus into the passage in Deuteronomy simply adds weight to the commandment.

How far could this process of manipulation go before a biblical book was so modified that it became another edition of the same book, or an entirely different book? Did books lose authority in the process?

Consider another example. I have already mentioned three different versions of the Pentateuch: the Masoretic Text, the Septuagint, and the Samaritan Pentateuch. The Masoretic Text is actually a medieval text, but it is based on manuscripts at least as old as the Dead Sea Scrolls; prototypes of the Masoretic Text (so-called proto-Masoretic or proto-rabbinic texts) have been found at Qumran. So have parts of various Hebrew

Agape with awe, Moses cradles one of the tablets bearing the Ten Commandments, while holding the other tablet in his raised hand, in "Moses with the Tablets of the Law" by Guido Reni (1575–1642).

The Nash Papyrus, acquired in Egypt in 1902 by W. L. Nash, was the oldest surviving biblical fragment before the discovery of the Dead Sea Scrolls. It probably dates to the second century B.C.E. The text contains the first portion of the Shema' ("Hear, O Israel, the LORD is our God, the LORD is one"), Judaism's affirmation of the unity of God.

JACOB GREETS LABAN

"Jacob greets Laban," by French artist Jean Restout (1692–1768). Having fled his home and the wrath of his brother Esau, youthful Jacob is welcomed into his uncle Laban's home, where he agrees to work for seven years in exchange for the hand of his younger cousin, Rebecca (at right). Years later, however, Jacob remains in his uncle's debt, having been tricked into first marrying his elder cousin, Leah (at left), then working another seven years for Rebecca. When Jacob has fulfilled his obligations and acquired a flock of his own, he tells his wives about a dream in which an angel told him "to arise, go forth from this land and return to the land of [his] fathers" (Genesis 31:4–13).

The question of whether Jacob fabricated this dream to justify his imminent departure is put to rest by the Samaritan Pentateuch.

base texts from which the Septuagint was translated. These are sometimes called "proto-Septuagintal." The Samaritan Pentateuch is a harmonized text like 4QDeuteronomy^n, as illustrated by the following example.

n the standard biblical text of Genesis 31:4–13, Jacob, who is still living with his father-in-law, Laban, tells his two wives, Rachel and Leah, about a dream he had long before, in which God commanded him to leave Aram and to return to Canaan. "During the mating of the flocks," Jacob rather abruptly recalls, "I once had a dream," in which a messenger of God told him "to arise, go forth from this land and return to the land of your fathers." This is the first we have heard of this dream. Did Jacob simply make it up to justify the pending departure to his wives? The Samaritan Pentateuch provides the answer.

Jacob's dream is first described in detail when he dreams it (after Genesis 30:36) and then later is repeated to his wives. The insertion reads as follows:

And the messenger of God spoke to Jacob in a dream, and he said "Jacob!" And he said "Here I am." And he said, "Raise your eyes and see all the he-goats climbing upon the flock, striped, speckled, tan, and spotted. For I have seen everything that Laban has done to you. I am the God of Bethel, where you anointed a pillar and vowed a vow to me. Now arise, go forth from this land and return to the land of your fathers, and I will deal well with you."

The language of the dream is exactly the same as Jacob's later report to his wives. Any doubts about Jacob's veracity in recounting the dream are laid to rest by including it in the biblical text.

This type of harmonization was used not just once but systematically throughout the entire Samaritan Pentateuch. When the Samaritan community adopted this edition as their canonical Torah, they also made certain sectarian changes. Instead of including the veiled references to Jerusalem and Mount Zion that appear in MT, the Samaritan Pentateuch refers to Shechem and Mount Gerizim, the Samaritan holy mountain. These are the places that God "has chosen," the Samaritan Pentateuch says. In MT, the parallel passages refer (obliquely) to Jerusalem and Mount Zion as the places that God "will choose." But before these sectarian changes were made and this edition was adopted by the Samaritan community, the harmonized Samaritan Pentateuch was in general circulation in Palestine. This is obvious from the fact that several copies of "proto-Samaritan" texts have been found at Qumran (for example, 4QNum[b] and 4QpaleoExod[m]).

At this time, and at least for some groups of Jews, there was no distinction between proto-Samaritan texts and proto-Masoretic texts; they were just different copies of the same authoritative book.

In sum, for the Sabbath command as well as the story of Jacob's dream, the scribal manipulations were extensive, but the passages are still recognizable as constituting the same biblical text. These are true harmonizations, which smooth over bumps in the text but do not add anything new. This kind of change does not seem to have altered the book's authority in any way. What would happen, though, if something brand new was added to the text?

This is just what occurs in several other Dead Sea Scroll manuscripts that are referred to as parabiblical or quasibiblical. Let us look at an example from one of these parabiblical texts, called 4QReworked Pentateuch. The complete document probably included the entire Pentateuch on one large scroll. Five manuscripts of the Reworked Pentateuch have been preserved, only one of which—designated 4Q365—we will look at here.[5] From the shape and form of the letters, 4Q365 can be dated to about 75 B.C.E.

As the title suggests, the scribe has reworked or changed the biblical text to a greater extent than we have seen with the Sabbath commandment or Jacob's dream. One type of change is the addition of brand new material. In 4Q365, a substantial addition was made to the Song of Miriam. In the standard biblical text, the Song of Miriam appears immediately following Moses' victory song at the Reed Sea (Exodus 15:1–18) and consists of just one sentence. Exodus 15:20–21 states:

> Then the prophet Miriam, Aaron's sister, took a tambourine in her hand; and all the women went out after her with tambourines and with dancing. And Miriam sang to them: "Sing to the LORD, for he has triumphed gloriously; horse and rider he has thrown into the sea."

Not only is Miriam's song short, but it is simply a repetition of the first line of the song of Moses in 15:1.[6]

But is that all that Miriam sang?

The Egyptians meet their fate as Miriam (far right, with tambourine) sings on, as depicted in this Armenian manuscript known as the Ritual Book, illustrated by Thoros Roslin in 1266. The Dead Sea Scroll manuscript known as 4QReworked Pentateuch adds seven lines to Miriam's song.

The answer in the Reworked Pentateuch is a resounding "No!" The additional text is fragmentary, but there is no doubt that it belongs here. After what we know as Exodus 15:21 and before 15:22, 4Q365 inserts seven additional lines to Miriam's song. The fragmentary addition goes like this:

1. **You despised**[7]
2. **for the majesty of**[
3. **You are great, a deliverer**[
4. **The hope of the enemy has perished, and he is for[gotten (or: has cea[sed)**
5. **they perished in the mighty waters, the enemy**[
6. **Extol the one who raises up, [a r]ansom … you gave**[
7. **[the one who do]es gloriously**[

Miriam's song is addressed to God and celebrates his victory over his enemies at the sea.[8] The additional text closes a perceived gap in the text and adds to the drama of the narrative, extending the theological message: God is the victor at the Reed Sea—not Moses or the Israelites. It interprets the text from within the text, making sure the reader understands the meaning of the story.[9] Thus the scribe was doing his job as the keeper of the tradition, making sure that the message was heard and properly understood by each new generation. This was not meant to be blasphemous or false. In fact, it was in the very act of reworking the text that the scribe indicated just how sacred or important the text actually was. An unimportant text would be discarded or forgotten; a sacred text like the Pentateuch, however, was constantly shaped and reshaped by generations of scribes and interpreters.

Would the first-century reader have recognized that this was an altered text of Exodus? Probably. Would

WHAT'S IN A NAME?

This view of Column X from the Habakkuk Commentary (IQpHab) shows a technique used by some Qumran scribes to treat the divine name. Whenever this scribe came to the name of the deity, he wrote out the four characters of the Tetragrammaton as he found them in the scriptural text, but he wrote them in the archaic slanted paleo-Hebrew script, rather than the newer square script he normally used.

Two examples can be seen in this photo. In line 7, the third word from the right, one can see the four letters of the Tetragrammaton (*yod, heh, vav, heh*) in a quotation from Habakkuk 2:13. The letters appear again in the last complete line, the second word from the left, in a quotation from Habakkuk 2:14. The verse reads: "For the earth will be filled with the knowledge of the Lord, as the waters cover the sea."

that have affected the authority of this Exodus text? We simply don't know. If it was considered acceptable to manipulate words in a text, as in the treatment of the Sabbath commandment in 4QDeuteronomy[n] or the addition to Jacob's dream in the Samaritan Pentateuch, why wouldn't the type of change in 4Q365—the addition to Miriam's song—be equally acceptable? If it were, 4Q365 would be just another manuscript of the Torah, equal in authority to any other manuscript.[10]

But I am not so sure about this. Two pieces of circumstantial evidence give me pause. First, this addition to Miriam's song did not continue to be copied in the late Second Temple period. Eventually it fell out of general circulation (at least we have no evidence of its continued use). Second, the unique passages in 4Q365 are not quoted elsewhere in Second Temple literature, with one exception.[11] Further, the vast body of rabbinic literature knows nothing of it. Clearly, 4Q365 was not widely known, certainly not beyond its own life as a manuscript. For that reason, I am inclined to think that, while 4Q365 may have had authority for a limited audience around the time of its production, it was never generally accepted as authoritative.

By the end of the first century C.E. we begin to see changes in the notion of both a canon, or list of sacred books, and an authoritative, unchangeable text. Josephus, the first-century Jewish historian, mentions a list of twenty-two sacred books (*Contra Apion* 1.37–43). His list implies that whatever is not included is not sacred. Similarly, 4 Ezra 14:45 talks about twenty-four "public" books that were written by divine inspiration (in addition to seventy "hidden" books known only to the wise).

With regard to the fixation of the text, a number of fragmentary biblical scrolls dating to the second century C.E., discovered in caves south of the Wadi Qumran, suggest that at about the time a canon was developing, so too was the notion of a fixed authoritative text. All of the second-century C.E. biblical manuscripts from the caves south of Qumran are proto-Masoretic texts; by this period, other text types seem to have fallen out of circulation. Thus, after the fall of the temple in 70 C.E., the canonical list becomes fixed in Palestinian Judaism, as does the text of those canonical books.[12] No deliberate changes would henceforth be made. A great tradition of innerbiblical exegesis—so clearly reflected in the Dead Sea Scrolls—had come to an end.

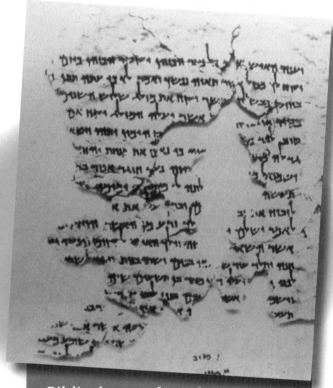

Biblical texts found at Qumran sometimes fill in gaps in the Masoretic Text. In this case a fragment from Samuel contains a paragraph from 1 Samuel 11 that was lost from the Masoretic Text by an error sometimes called *homeoteleuton*—when the scribe's eye moved from one word to a later appearance of the same word, skipping text in between.

THE "LOST" FRAGMENT OF SAMUEL

The passage depicted on the opposite page solves a mystery in 1 Samuel 11. In this story an Ammonite king named Nahash besieges the Israelite city of Jabesh-Gilead. The Israelites agree to surrender and serve the Ammonites, hoping thereby to save their lives. Nahash agrees on the condition that the right eyes of the Israelites be gouged out, to humiliate them. This seemingly unmotivated cruelty was not the usual treatment of conquered subjects and is unexplained in the Masoretic Text. Mutilation was usually reserved for certain classes of offenders, including rebels. From the Dead Sea Scroll text, we now know that after defeat in previous battles with the Ammonites 7,000 Israelite warriors had fled to Jabesh-Gilead, where they were given refuge. Thus, in effect, Jabesh-Gilead was a rebel city. That was the reason for Nahash's threat. Incidentally, Saul came to the rescue of the city and saved the Jabesh-Gileadites.

NOTES

1. Sidnie White Crawford, "4QDeut[n]," in *Discoveries in the Judaean Desert XIV* (ed. Eugene Ulrich et al.; Oxford: Clarendon, 1995), 117–128, plates 28–29.

2. Emanuel Tov, "The Nature and Background of Harmonizations in Biblical Manuscripts," *Journal for the Study of the Old Testament* 31 (1985): 3–29.

3. I say "probably" because, unfortunately, the Sabbath commandment has not been preserved in any other Qumran manuscript of Exodus or Deuteronomy, although it does appear in the phylactery (*tephillin*) texts.

4. Eugene Ulrich, "The Bible in the Making: The Scriptures at Qumran," in *The Community of the Renewed Covenant* (ed. Eugene Ulrich and James VanderKam; Notre Dame, Ind.: University of Notre Dame Press, 1996), 84.

5. Emanuel Tov and Sidnie White (Crawford), "Reworked Pentateuch," in *Discoveries in the Judaean Desert XIII* (ed. James VanderKam et al.; Oxford: Clarendon, 1994), 187–352, plates 13–36. Tov and I argued that these five manuscripts—4Q158, 4Q364, 4Q365, 4Q366, and 4Q367—were all copies of a single composition. Recently Michael Segal argued that they are separate compositions. See his "4QReworked Pentateuch or 4QPentateuch?" in *The Dead Sea Scrolls Fifty Years After Their Discovery: Proceedings of the Jerusalem Congress, July 20–25, 1997* (ed. Lawrence H. Schiffman, Emanuel Tov, and James VanderKam; Jerusalem: Israel Exploration Society, 2000). The resolution of this question is not important for our purposes here.

6. For this reason, some scholars believe Moses' song was originally Miriam's song. See Phyllis Trible, "Bringing Miriam Out of the Shadows," *Bible Review* 5.1 (1989): 14–25, 34.

7. The open bracket indicates that the end of the line of text is missing in the fragmentary scroll. Reconstructed text also appears in brackets.

8. For discussion of the contents of the song, see George Brooke, "Power to the Powerless—A Long-Lost Song of Miriam," *Biblical Archaeology Review* 20.3 (1994): 62–65.

9. This is called "innerbiblical exegesis." See Michael Fishbane, *Biblical Interpretation in Ancient Israel* (Oxford: Clarendon, 1985).

10. This is the position of Ulrich ("The Qumran Scrolls and the Biblical Text," in Schiffman, Tov, and VanderKam, *The Dead Sea Scrolls*).

11. The Qumran Temple Scroll may quote a passage in Leviticus from 4Q365. See Tov and White, "4Q365," in VanderKam et al., *Discoveries in the Judaean Desert XIII*, 290–96.

12. Debates about which books belonged in the canon went on for some time. Esther did not gain universal acceptance until the third century C.E. There are also different canons for different groups: the Hebrew Bible, Septuagint and Old Testament are all different, although with much overlap.

A remarkable view from the mouth of one of the many caves that pock the hills rising above it. This terrace provides a commanding view of the Dead Sea shore about a kilometer to the east.

A VIEW FROM THE TOP

Approximately one-half mile south of Cave 1, a roughly triangular terrace juts out from the Judean hills above the narrow coastal plain. From the terrace one can also see a good distance to the north toward Jericho — a view, it seems, from the top of the world!

The wall ruins that can be seen on the surface of the terrace had been known for years and were identified on survey maps as Khirbet Qumran. *Khirbet* means "ruins" in Arabic; Qumran is the name of the wadi cut by water runoff through the Judean hills, which issues onto the coastal plain just south of the marl terrace, to the right in this view.

THE SCROLLS AND EARLY CHRISTIANITY

How They Are Related and What They Share

By James C. VanderKam

Almost from the moment the first Dead Sea Scrolls came under scholarly scrutiny, the question of their relation to early Christianity became a key issue. The early days of Qumran research produced some spectacular theories regarding the relationship among Jesus, the first Christians, and the Qumran community. In 1950 the French scholar André Dupont-Sommer argued that the Teacher of Righteousness—the founder and first leader of the Qumran group, according to the scrolls—had a career that prefigured and paralleled that of Jesus:

> The Galilean Master, as He is presented to us in the writings of the New Testament, appears in many respects as an astonishing reincarnation of the Master of Justice [Teacher of Righteousness]. Like the latter He preached penitence, poverty, humility, love of one's neighbor, chastity. Like him, He prescribed the observance of the Law of Moses, the whole Law, but the Law finished and perfected, thanks to His own revelations. Like him He was the Elect and Messiah of God, the Messiah redeemer of the world. Like him He was the object of the hostility of the priests, the party of the Sadducees. Like him He was condemned and put to death. Like him he pronounced judgment on Jerusalem, which was taken and destroyed by the Romans for having put Him to death. Like him, at the end of time, He will be the supreme judge. Like him he founded a church whose adherents fervently awaited His glorious return.[1]

Dupont-Sommer's speculations strongly influenced Edmund Wilson, author of a *New Yorker* article that stimulated great popular interest in and controversy about the scrolls.[2] Wilson argued that the relation of the covenanters of Qumran to Jesus and the first Christians could be seen as "the successive phases of a movement."[3] Wilson wrote, "The monastery, this structure of stone that endures, between the bitter waters and precipitous cliffs, with its oven and its inkwells, its mill and its cesspool, its constellation of sacred fonts and the unadorned graves of its dead, is perhaps, more than Bethlehem or Nazareth, the cradle of Christianity."[4]

According to Wilson, Jewish and Christian scholars were reluctant to admit the implications of the scrolls because of their religious biases. Jewish scholars were supposedly anxious lest the authority of the Masoretic Text (the traditional Jewish text of the Hebrew Bible) be shaken, especially by the variant readings in the Biblical texts found at Qumran. Jews would also be uncomfortable, he suggested, if Christianity were seen, as the scrolls indicated, as a natural development from a particular brand of Judaism. Christianity too was supposedly threatened by the content of the scrolls: the uniqueness of Christ was imperiled. In an oft-quoted passage, the iconoclastic Wilson concluded:

It would seem an immense advantage for cultural and social intercourse—that is, for civilization—that the rise of Christianity should, at last, be generally understood as simply an episode of human history rather than propagated as dogma and divine revelation. The study of the Dead Sea Scrolls—with the direction it is now taking—cannot fail, one would think, to conduce this.[5]

At the same time, other scholars were going about the patient labor of establishing just where the points of contact and difference were. Millar Burrows of Yale, for example, embraced a minimalist thesis in his widely used *The Dead Sea Scrolls*.[6] Against those who claimed the scrolls would revolutionize New Testament study, he wrote:

There is no danger ... that our understanding of the New Testament will be so revolutionized by the Dead Sea Scrolls as to require a revision of any basic article of Christian faith. All scholars who have worked on the texts will agree that this has not happened and will not happen.[7]

In a less pastoral vein, Burrows stated his view of the relationship between the Qumran sect and early Christians in these words:

Direct influence of the Qumran sect on the early church may turn out to be less probable than parallel developments in the same general situation. The question here is the same one encountered when we attempt to explain similarities between Judaism and Zoroastrianism, or between Christianity and the pagan mystery cults.[8]

A MANUAL OF IMPORTANCE

This important scroll, initially called by scholars the Manual of Discipline, contains rules and regulations for a devout separatist Jewish group. The manual was one of several sectarian documents, writings clearly produced by a particular group of a religious sect for use by the members, found among the Dead Sea Scrolls.

Eventually, fragments of about ten copies of the Manual of Discipline were retrieved from Cave 4 and fragments of at least one more from Cave 5. The Manual of Disciple scroll was important to scholars because it strengthened the argument that the scrolls were placed in the caves by members of an organized religious settlement and identified some of the distinctive practices of that group.

As matters developed, this view has largely set the general framework within which the relationship between Qumran and Christianity is still understood today. Many Qumran scholars would agree with Burrows's conclusion:

> After studying the Dead Sea Scrolls for seven years, I do not find my understanding of the New Testament substantially affected. Its Jewish background is clearer and better understood but its meaning has neither been changed nor significantly clarified.[9]

In *The Scrolls and the New Testament,* Krister Stendahl collected thirteen detailed studies of the sect by eleven different scholars examining the major similarities between the Qumran sect and early Christianity.[10] None of Dupont-Sommer's writings was selected for inclusion. In his perceptive introductory essay, Stendahl concluded, "It is true to say that the Scrolls add to the background of Christianity, but they add so much that we arrive at a point where the significance of similarities definitely rescues Christianity from false claims of originality in the popular sense and leads us back to a new grasp of its true foundation in the person and the events of its Messiah."[11]

Jewish Apocalyptic Tradition at Qumran and in Christianity

One of the most influential books about Qumran was written by Frank M. Cross of Harvard. In *The Ancient Library of Qumran and Modern Biblical Studies,* Cross lays special stress on the Essenes (a Jewish movement of which the Qumran group was a part) as bearers and producers of the Jewish apocalyptic tradition and on the importance of this tradition for early Christianity:

This photograph shows the view looking out of Cave 4 toward the coastal plain to the south (made green by the nearby *'Ain Feshkha* spring) and beyond the plain to the Dead Sea.

The background of the institutions and patterns typical of the communal life of the earliest Church in an earlier apocalyptic milieu can now be investigated seriously for the first time, The Essene literature [from Qumran] enables us to discover the concrete Jewish setting in which an apocalyptic understanding of history was living and integral to communal existence. Like the primitive Church, the Essene community was distinguished from Pharisaic associations and other movements within Judaism precisely in its consciousness "of being already the called and chosen Congregation of the end of days."[12] Contrary to the tendency of New Testament theologians to assume that the "eschatological existence" of the early Church, that is, its community life lived in anticipation of the Kingdom of God, together with the forms shaped by this life, was a uniquely Christian phenomenon, we must now affirm that in the Essene communities we discover antecedents of Christian forms and concepts.[13]

Within this general framework Cross then considers parallels in three areas: in *theological language* (especially in John), in *eschatological motifs* (especially in the way Scripture was interpreted to refer to their own time, but also in their understanding of themselves as people of the new covenant and in their messianic outlook), and in their *order and liturgical institutions* (baptism, liturgical meals, community of goods, leadership). In each case the Qumran covenanters and early Christians shared essential viewpoints.

In 1966 Herbert Braun published a work entitled *Qumran und das Neue Testament* containing a chainlike treatment of all New Testament passages, from Matthew through Revelation, for which a Qumran parallel arguably exists.[14] The book totals 326 pages of rather small print. Naturally these parallels vary in quality and importance, but, whatever the limits of the collection, the sheer quantity is certainly impressive.

In sum, as Qumran research has matured, it has been widely recognized that, although there were major differences between the Qumran literature and early Christian literature and between the Qumran community and the early Christian community, nevertheless, they were also remarkably similar in theological vocabulary, in some major doctrinal tenets, and in several organizational and ritual practices. Yet most scholars were reluctant to explain early Christian teachings as direct borrowings from Qumran Essenism. The better view is that the two are offspring of a common tradition in Judaism, with perhaps some points of direct borrowing (especially organizational ones).[15] As more of the scrolls have been published, this general conclusion has been substantially sustained.

A BIRD'S-EYE VIEW

This aerial view of Qumran reveals the full groundplan of the building complex. The higher walls at the upper left are the remains of a tower. In the long room directly to the right of the tower were found fragments of a plaster table and bench, along with two inkwells. It has been argued that the second-story room above was a scriptorium in which religious scrolls were copied. The long rectangular room at the upper right, the largest room, probably was a communal dining hall.

True, even today a scholar here and there departs from this mainline view. For example, Robert Eisenman of California State University at Long Beach has posited a Zadokite movement, of which the Qumran community was a part, that supposedly existed for centuries and included Ezra, Judas Maccabee, John the Baptist, Jesus, and his brother James;[16] only in the first century C.E. did this movement become a separate group and compose the sectarian documents of Qumran. Barbara Thiering of the University of Sydney in Australia has identified John the Baptist as the Teacher of Righteousness and Jesus as the Wicked Priest of the Qumran texts.[17] J. L. Teicher of Cambridge University argues, on the other hand, that the apostle Paul is the Wicked Priest.[18] Few, if any, scholars have been convinced by the arguments adduced by Eisenman, Thiering, or Teicher, but the popular press has sometimes given their sensational views widespread coverage.[19]

What Qumran Texts Teach Us About The New Testament

Let's look more closely at some of the significant similarities between the New Testament and the Qumran literature and assess them. But before doing so, two thoughts should be expressed.

First, we must appreciate the insights provided by the Qumran literature in light of the paucity of any other Hebrew or Aramaic literature contemporary with the beginnings of Christianity. The books of the Hebrew Bible are, in almost all cases, considerably earlier. The vast corpus of rabbinic texts was written centuries later. Before the Qumran discoveries, most of the first-century comparative material for studying early Christianity came from Greek and Latin sources. The sudden availability of an entire library of Hebrew and Aramaic texts dating from approximately the time of

the New Testament events has naturally, and rightfully, captured the attention of New Testament scholars.

Second, proving direct dependence of something in the New Testament on an item in the scrolls is no simple task. Even now we know very little about the various groups of Jews in the last centuries of the Second Temple period. (The Second Temple was destroyed by the Romans in 70 C.E.) Even if we show that the only places where a particular item or concept is found are the New Testament and the Qumran texts, this would not prove either a direct borrowing or that the feature was unique to these two groups. The feature may have been shared more widely, with most of its attestation now lost. Given these limitations, we can, at most, do little more than isolate areas where Christians and Essenes agreed and all other known groups seem to have disagreed.

One of the clearest examples of the insights the Qumran literature can provide for New Testa-

ment literature relates to language and verbal formulas. The New Testament is written in Greek. Jesus, however, spoke Aramaic, and all of the first disciples were Semitic-speaking Jews of Galilee or Judea. The Qumran texts now supply us, for the first time, with the original Hebrew (and sometimes Aramaic) of a number of New Testament words and phrases.

Consider, for example, the Greek expression *tōn pleiōn*, which is usually translated "many" or "majority." This is a very general term that became, in several New Testament passages, a designation for entire groups of Jesus' followers (Matthew 26:28; see also Mark 14:24; Luke 22:20; Acts 6:2, 5; 15:12, 30; and 2 Corinthians 2:5–6). For example, Paul writes to the Corinthians: "But if anyone has caused pain, he has caused it not to me, but in some measure—not to put it too severely—to you all. For such a one as this punishment by the majority [*tōn pleiōn*] is enough" (2 Corinthians 2:5–6). The Qumran scroll known as the Manual of Discipline (1QS) contains rules regarding who may speak and when during general meetings of the group: "And in an Assembly of the Congregation no man shall speak without the consent of the Congregation, nor indeed of the Guardian of the Congregation" (Manual of Discipline 6:11–12).[20] The Hebrew word translated "congregation" in this passage is *hrbym* (vocalized, with vowels, as *harabbîm*), which literally means "the many." In other words, *hrbym* is the Hebrew word that lies behind the New Testament Greek phrase *tōn pleiōn*.

This ritual purification bath, or *mikveh*, once contained a pool of water used to purify and sanctify a person for various religious purposes.

There may be another example in this same passage. The Hebrew word rendered "guardian" (*hmbqr*) in this passage (and others where it refers to a man who has a supervisory role in the Qumran community[21]) may be the equivalent of *episkopos* (bishop/overseer), which is used several times in the New Testament (Philippians 1:1; 1 Timothy 3:1–7; Titus 1:7), where it also refers to a man with a similar role.

With the help of the Dead Sea Scrolls, we can uncover the Hebrew or Aramaic originals of several other expressions in the New Testament, not only in the Gospels but in the Pauline corpus as well. Joseph Fitzmyer, of the Catholic University of America in Washington, D.C., has identified the Semitic original of a number of Pauline expressions of this kind, such as the following: "the righteousness of God" (*dikaiosyne theou = sidqat 'ēl*), "works of the law" (*erga nomou = ma'ăsê tôrāh*), "the church of God" (*hē ekklēsia tou theou = qĕhal 'ēl*), and "Sons of Light" (*huloi phōtos = bĕnê 'ôr*).[22]

Gospel Fragments at Qumran?

Can we go further? Is it possible that a fragment of a Gospel has been found at Qumran? The Qumran settlement was destroyed by the Romans in 68 C.E. Many believe that by this date Mark, the earliest of the canonical Gospels, had been composed. So it is not beyond the realm of possibility that a Gospel text would turn up at Qumran. Indeed, one scholar has claimed to have identified several scraps from Qumran Cave 7, where Greek fragments were found, as containing not only parts of the text of Mark, but also Acts, Romans, 1 Timothy, James, and 2 Peter. José O'Callaghan, a Spanish Jesuit scholar, created a worldwide sensation in the 1970s when he made this proposal, but today his thesis has generally been abandoned. The scraps on which O'Callaghan relied are tiny, nearly illegible texts that seem not to agree entirely with the relevant texts even for the few letters that can be read. Naturally, if O'Callaghan's identification were correct, it would require major changes in the generally accepted theories about who the residents of Qumran were, at least in the later phases of the settlement.

Although no actual copies of New Testament books have been found at Qumran, parts of some New Testament books may have been drawn from Qumran or Essene sources and then revised and edited into their present contexts. Consider, for example, 2 Corinthians 6:14–15:

Do not be unequally yoked together with unbelievers. For what fellowship has righteousness with lawlessness? And what communion has light with darkness? And what accord has Christ with Belial? Or what part has a believer with an unbeliever?

The entire passage sounds very much like what we find at Qumran, including the contrast between light and darkness and the strong consciousness of being an exclusive group. The name Belial (or Beliar) occurs only here in the whole New Testament, but it occurs several times at Qumran: in the Hymns Scroll and in the unpublished halakhic letter known as 4QMMT, as well as elsewhere. We cannot prove that this passage from 2 Corinthians is a revised Essene text, but Paul uses language here that is known elsewhere only from Qumran texts.[23]

A similar claim can be made about the Sermon on the Mount in Matthew 5–7. It, too, includes a number of expressions that are attested at Qumran but nowhere else. For example, the "poor in spirit" (Matthew 5:3) is found in the War of the Sons of Light against the Sons of Darkness (14:7) but in no other ancient text. Likewise, the sermon's teaching that oaths should be avoided as unnecessary, since one's word should suffice (Matthew 5:33–37), echoes the emphasis on truth in the scrolls (Manual of Discipline 2:24, 26, for example, calls the group "the community of truth") and may even explain Josephus's remark that the Essenes were excused from taking the oath of loyalty to Herod.[24]

In addition, the duty to turn the other cheek (Matthew 5:38–39) is found at Qumran in the Manual of Discipline (10:17–18),[25] but not elsewhere. Finally, the antitheses in the Sermon on the Mount ("You have heard that it was said…, but I say unto you…") are reminiscent of the way in which the halakhic letter 4QMMT introduces disagreements between the sect and its opponents: "You know…. We think/say…."

> It has been widely recognized that, although there were major differences between Qumran literature and early Christian literature and their respective communities, they were also remarkably similar in theological vocabulary, in some major doctrinal tenets, and in several organizational and ritual practices.

Early Christians at Qumran?

Not surprisingly, the question has arisen as to whether some New Testament characters can be placed at Qumran. As we have seen, Dupont-Sommer long ago argued that the Teacher of Righteousness, who figures so prominently in the Qumran documents, prefigured Jesus. However, even he does not equate the two. I have also mentioned the widely rejected view that Jesus' brother James the Just (proposed by Eisenman) and the apostle Paul (proposed by Teicher) appear in the scrolls.

The most likely candidate to have had contact with the Qumran community, however, is John the Baptist. From the beginning, scholars have been intrigued by the similarities between John and his teachings, on the one hand, and Qumran and its doctrines, on the other. The Baptist is therefore the prime candidate for contact with Qumran. The contention is not without some force.

John the Baptist came from a priestly family (Luke 1:5). At his birth his father said of him:

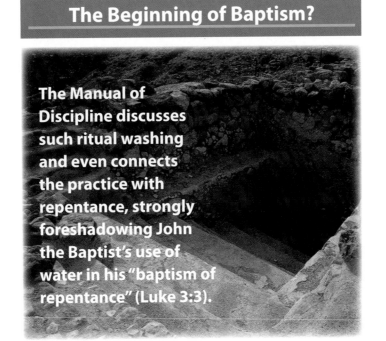

The Beginning of Baptism?

The Manual of Discipline discusses such ritual washing and even connects the practice with repentance, strongly foreshadowing John the Baptist's use of water in his "baptism of repentance" (Luke 3:3).

"And you, child, will be called the prophet of the Most High; for you will go before the Lord to prepare his ways, to give knowledge of salvation to his people in the forgiveness of sins, through the tender mercy of our God, when the day shall dawn upon us from on high." (Luke 1:76–78)

Luke then adds:

The child grew and became strong, in spirit, and he was in the wilderness till the day of his manifestation to Israel. (Luke 1.80)

This particular wilderness is the Wilderness of Judea near the Jordan River, which flows into the Dead Sea very near Qumran (Luke 3:3; see also Matthew 3:1, 5–6; Mark 1:4–5).

Accordingly, John lived in the Wilderness of Judea before his ministry began, and it was there that the word of God came to him in the fifteenth year of the emperor Tiberias (Luke 3:1–2). All three Synoptic Gospels introduce John's public ministry in similar fashion by noting that his was a preaching of repentance (Matthew 3:2; Mark 1:4; Luke 3:3). In the passage in Luke, he is described as "preaching a baptism of repentance for the forgiveness of sins" (Luke: 3:3). We are told that his preaching had a larger purpose in the divine plan for the latter days, since it fulfilled the words of Isaiah: John is "the voice of one crying in the wilderness: 'Prepare the way of the Lord, make his paths straight. Every valley shall be filled, and every mountain and hill shall be brought low, and the crooked shall be made straight, and the rough places shall be made smooth; and all flesh shall see the salvation of God.'" Luke (3:3–6) is here quoting Isaiah 40:3–4. Matthew 3:3 and Mark 1:2–3 also quote this passage, although not at such length. John's preaching is characterized by an eschatological urgency, by the need for repentance before

the great day dawns and the Lord comes.

Both Matthew and Mark append a description of John's unusual clothing and diet: he wore a camel's hair vestment with a leather belt and ate locusts and wild honey (Matthew 3:4; Mark 1:6). All three Synoptic Gospels specify that John's baptizing took place in the Jordan River (Matthew 3:5–6; Mark 1:5; Luke

RIVER FOR REPENTANCE

We know from the New Testament that the region where the Jordan River approaches the Dead Sea had achieved special spiritual significance by the last century of the Second Temple period (first century C.E.).

According to the Gospels, John the Baptist chose the Jordan River, somewhere near this spot, to preach the imminent coming of the day of judgment and the need for repentance and purification, and he used the waters of the Jordan for ritual ablution to signify religious cleansing (Matthew 3:1–12; Mark 1:2–8; Luke 3:1–17). These were also dominant concerns in the life and literature of the Qumran community.

The traditional site of John's baptisms, shown here, is approximately four miles north of the Dead Sea and less than eight miles northeast of Qumran.

3:3). His imperative message stirred the people, as John forthrightly brought people's sins to their attention (Matthew 3:7–10; Luke 3:7–14). Luke reports that John himself became the object of his audience's interest: "The people were in expectation and all men questioned in their hearts concerning John, whether perhaps he were the Christ [that is, the messiah]" (Luke 3:15). At this point he proclaims the coming of a greater one who would baptize, not with water as John did, but with the Holy Spirit and with fire, one who would come for judgment (Luke 3:16–18; see also Matthew 3:11–12; Mark 1:7–8; John 1:19–28). John later baptized Jesus (Matthew 3:13–15; Mark 1:8; Luke 3:21) and was eventually imprisoned and executed (see Matthew 14:1–12).

A great deal of this picture is reminiscent of the Qumran community. John's geographical location seems to have been very close to Qumran. The Gospel of John locates his baptizing ministry "in Bethany beyond the Jordan" (John 1:28) and "at Aenon near Salim, because there was plenty of water" (John 3:23). Neither of these sites is known with certainty, but they seem to have lain somewhat north of

Qumran. Yet the fact that he worked in the wilderness near the Jordan could well have brought him to the vicinity of, or even to, Qumran. The baptism of repentance that John administered parallels the Qumran teaching about washing in water for cleansing and sanctification (Manual of Discipline 3:4–5, 9). According to another passage in the same Qumran text (5:13–14): "They shall not enter the water to partake of the pure Meal of the saints, for they shall not be cleansed, unless they turn from their wickedness: for all who transgress His word are unclean."

The Qumran settlement includes a number of cisterns, some of which were used for the frequent ritual baths of those who belonged to the community. There were probably differences between the baptism of John and the Qumran rituals (John's baptism may have occurred just once for each penitent; the Qumran ablutions seem to have been more frequent), but both were connected with repentance and, unlike proselyte baptism, were meant for Jews. It should also be recalled that both the Qumran community and John the Baptist have their missions explained in our records by the same scriptural citation: Isaiah 40:3. The Manual of Discipline (8:12–15) quotes this verse to indicate that the group believed it was fulfilling the prophet's words by going literally into the wilderness to prepare the way of the Lord through study of Moses' Torah. The various similarities between the Qumran sect and John add up to something less than an identification of John as an Essene but are certainly suggestive and lead some to make such claims about this New Testament forerunner.[26] On the other hand,

Fractured by an earthquake in 31 B.C.E., steps about six feet wide lead into a large, heavily plastered *miqveh*. Built by the Essenes at Qumran in the second century B.C.E., the roofless pool was originally identified as a cistern for this Judean wilderness community.

if John was a member of the Qumran community, he must have later separated from it to pursue his independent, solitary ministry.

New Light on Melchizedek as Jesus' Forebear

Another New Testament personality on whom several Qumran texts in fact cast a new light is Melchizedek. He appears a number of times in the New Testament book referred to as the Letter to the Hebrews as a priest to whose order Jesus belonged. The Gospel genealogies, however, show that Jesus was not a member of the tribe of Levi, from which the priests came. In these genealogies, Jesus is descended from David (Matthew 1:1–17; Luke 3:23–38). In his attempt to portray the Davidic Jesus as a priest, the author of Hebrews elaborates traditions about the mysterious priest-king Melchizedek of Salem, who appears in Genesis. There Melchizedek meets Abram and blesses the patriarch (Genesis 14:18–20). In the following quotation from Hebrews 7:1–3, the first sentence accurately describes what happened in Genesis; the remainder elaborates this text and joins it with a sentence in Psalm 110:4:

> For this Melchizedek, king of Salem, priest of the Most High God, met Abraham returning from the slaughter of the kings and blessed him; and to him Abraham apportioned a tenth part of everything [of the booty]. He is first, by translation of his name, king of righteousness, and then he is also king of Salem, that is, king of peace. He is without father or mother or genealogy, and has neither beginning of days nor end of life, but resembling the Son of God he continues a priest forever.

The author of Hebrews fashions an extraordinary portrait of Melchizedek, based on inferences (for example, his eternity, his superiority to Levi) from a combination of Genesis 14:18–20 and Psalm 110:4 (which he quotes at Hebrews 7:17).

A Qumran text appropriately labeled 11 QMelchizedek now provides at least something of a parallel to the exalted status and characteristics of Melchizedek in Hebrews. In the Qumran text Melchizedek is pre-

sented as an angelic being who raises up God's holy ones for deeds of judgment and who takes divine vengeance on evil. Here Melchizedek has superhuman status, which clearly involves living eternally just as in Hebrews.

More recently, another Qumran text was published that appears to mention Melchizedek: the Songs of the Sabbath Sacrifice.[27] Although the relevant fragments

SONGS OF THE SABBATH

This scroll fragment found in one of the casemate rooms at Masada is identical in two respects to a document uncovered at Qumran. The Masada fragment is sometimes called the Songs of the Sabbath Service because these songs are to be used on particular Sabbaths. Fragments of other copies of the same document were found among the materials recovered from Qumran Cave 4.

are poorly preserved, Melchizedek seems to officiate as the heavenly high priest, just as Jesus does in Hebrews.

To this point we have surveyed the theories of scholars, some of them bold and some cautious, about the possible relationship between the Qumran texts, Jesus, and the New Testament. For the most part, we have looked at the Qumran texts for what they can teach us about New Testament language, for their striking parallels with New Testament passages, and to ask whether some of the same characters may walk both stages. Now we focus our attention on certain important elements that the Dead Sea Scrolls and Christianity share.

Ritual and Community Practices

Many of the ritual and community practices of the Qumran covenanters who lived near the Dead Sea and who produced what we call the Dead Sea Scrolls have impressive parallels among New Testament Christians. Here are just a few.

Acts describes the events of the first Pentecost after Jesus' crucifixion. It then describes the property the community holds in common: "And all who believed were together and had all things in common; and they sold their possessions and goods and distributed them to all, as any had need" (Acts 2:44–45; see also Acts 4:32).

Later, in Acts 5:1–11, Luke narrates the celebrated case of Ananias and Sapphira, who sold some land but presented to the community only a part of the proceeds. Peter accuses them of withholding, and they both fall down dead. Here Acts is reflecting

GROUP GATHERING PLACES

This room (left) was filled with stacks of basic pottery eating vessels. More than a thousand crude bowls, dishes, small jars and jugs were found in the room—enough to serve a sizable gathering.

Long rooms such as the one to the right were dubbed *refectories* after the term for the dining rooms in later Christian monasteries.

the situation in the early Christian community in Jerusalem. Paul, on the other hand, writes as if members of the churches that he founded had private means with which to contribute to the needs of others (for example, 1 Corinthians 16:2). Moreover, even in Jerusalem, contribution to the community may have been voluntary, for Acts 5:4 states: "After [the property] was sold, were not the proceeds at your disposal?" If so, the sin of Ananias and Sapphira was not withholding, but making a partial donation of the proceeds while giving the impression that it was the whole.

The Manual of Discipline from Qumran makes several allusions to the merging of members' private property with the possessions of the group. This theme is especially prominent in the section that describes initiatory procedures for potential members. At first the novice is not allowed to share the pure meal of the congregation, "nor shall he have any share of the property of the Congregation" (6:17). Once he has completed a full year within the group and it is determined that he may remain, "his property and earnings shall be handed over to the Bursar of the Congregation who shall register it to his account [but] shall not spend it for the Congregation" (6:19–20). Only after an additional, successful year of probation is it stipulated that "his property shall be merged" with the community's possessions (6:22). The practice is compulsory at Qumran and follows full admission to the congregation.[28]

A sacred meal with eschatological significance also seems to be something that the Qumran covenanters and the early Christians shared.

The Last Supper, which Jesus shared with his immediate followers, is presented in two ways in the Gospels. For Matthew, Mark, and Luke, it is a Passover meal complete with bread and wine; for John, however, it was eaten the night before Passover, and neither bread nor wine is mentioned. In the Passover version of the Last Supper, bread and wine play prominent roles; indeed, they attain a sacramental significance:

> Now as they were eating, Jesus took the bread, and blessed, and broke it, and gave it to the disciples and said, "Take, eat; this is my body." And he took a cup, and when he had given thanks he gave it to them, saying,

"Drink of it, all of you; for this is my blood of the covenant, which is poured out for many for the forgiveness of sins. I tell you I shall not drink again of this fruit of the vine until that day when I drink it new with you in my Father's kingdom." (Matthew 26:26–29; see also Mark 14:22–25; Luke 22:17–20).

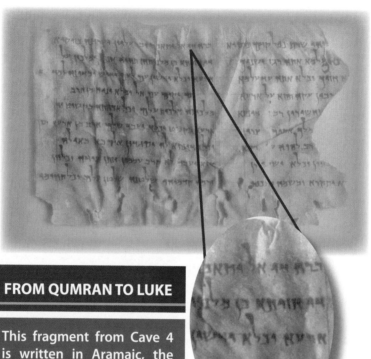

FROM QUMRAN TO LUKE

This fragment from Cave 4 is written in Aramaic, the spoken language of Judean Jews in the last centuries before the fall of Jerusalem. The text is probably part of a sectarian document used, and perhaps also produced, by the Qumran community.

Special attention has been drawn to this scrap of text because in it the titles "son of God" and "son of the Most High" appear in a context that seems close to the way those titles are applied to Jesus in the New Testament Gospel of Luke.

These words give special meaning to the physical elements of the meal and place the ceremony within a context of expectation for "that day when I drink it new with you in my Father's kingdom."

The Qumran texts, too, describe a special meal that involved the basic elements of bread and wine. The Manual of Discipline refers to the meals of the group: "And when the table has been prepared for eating, and the new wine for drinking, the Priest shall be the first to stretch out his hand to bless the first-fruits of the bread and new wine" (6:4–6).[29]

This same text also mentions a "pure meal" that only those who have passed through a year-long probationary period were permitted to eat (6:16–17); they were not allowed to partake of the "drink of the congregation" until a second such year had passed (6:20–21). Finally, those who were guilty of slandering another member of the community were excluded from this meal for one year (7:16).

The clearest statement about a special meal at Qumran comes from the Rule of the Congregation (1QSa), which, was originally part of the Manual of Discipline:

[The ses]sion of the men of renown, [invited to] the feast for the council of the community when [at the end] (of days) the messiah [shall assemble] with them. [The priest] shall enter [at] the head of all the congregation of Israel, and [all his brethren the sons of] Aaron, the priests, [who are invited] to the feast, the men of renown, and they shall sit be[fore him, each] according to his importance. Afterwards [the messiah] of Israel [shall enter]

SIGNIFICANCE

and the heads of the [thousands of Israel] shall sit before him [ea]ch according to his importance, according to [his station] in their encampments and their journeys. And all of the heads of the [households of the congrega]tion, [their] sag[es and wise men,] shall sit before them, each according to his importance. [When they] mee[t at the] communal [tab]le, [to set out bread and wi]ne, and the communal table is arranged [to eat and] to dri[nk] wine [no] one [shall extend] his hand to the first (portion) of the bread and [the wine] before the priest. Fo[r he shall] bless the first (portion) of the bread and the wi[ne and shall extend] his hand to the bread first. Afterwa[rds,] the messiah of Israel [shall exten]d his hands to the bread. [Afterwards,] all of the congregation of the community [shall ble]ss, ea[ch according to] his importance. [They] shall act according to this statute whenever (the meal) is ar[ranged] when as many as ten [meet] together.[30] (Rule of the Congregation 2:11–22)

This special meal, eaten in the presence of the two messiahs postulated at Qumran, was only for the ritually pure (compare 1 Corinthians 11:27–29).

Lawrence Schiffman, of New York University, argues that the Qumran meals were nonsacral or cultic in nature; rather, "these meals, conducted regularly as part of the present-age way of life of the sect, were preenactments of the final messianic banquet which the sectarians expected in the soon-to-come end of days. Again, the life of the sect in this world mirrored its dreams for the age to come."[31] But however the meal of the Qumran covenanters is interpreted, its messianic character, the prominence of bread and wine, the fact that it was repeated regularly, and the explicit eschatological associations do in fact remind one of elements found in the New Testament words about the Lord's Last Supper.[32]

Jesus' Crucifixion in Relation to Passover

According to at least one scholar, the Qumran texts may provide a solution to an old calendrical problem in Gospel studies.[33] The Synoptic Gospels (Matthew, Mark, and Luke), on the one hand, and John, on the other, place the Last Supper on different dates. The Synoptics place the Last Supper on a Friday and treat it as a Passover meal; John, however, puts it on a Thursday, the day before Passover, and dates Jesus' death to the next day—at a time when the Passover lambs were being slaughtered. The official Hebrew calendar used in the Jerusalem temple was a lunar calendar with some solar adjustments. At Qumran, the covenanters used a 364-day solar calendar. A French scholar, Annie Jaubert, has proposed that, since two calendars were used in Judaism at this time, it is possible that the Synoptic writers followed one calendar (the solar calendar) and that John followed the official lunar calendar.[34]

Some have found this solution attractive, but there is no evidence that the writers of the Gospels followed different calendrical systems. Moreover, it is evident that John had a larger purpose in mind in arranging events in the passion week as he did. John does not emphasize the bread and wine at Jesus' meal; they are not even mentioned. Instead, foot-washing and mutual love are highlighted. By dying when he did in John's chronology, Jesus is presented as the Passover lamb of his people, slaughtered the following day.

THE "SON OF GOD" SCROLL

In a fragment (opposite page) from Qumran, the title "son of God" is applied to a future divine savior, and both forms of the title, "son of God" and "son of the Most High," are used as in Luke's account of Gabriel's announcement to Mary. The verb used in this fragment in both places is translated the same as in Luke: "he shall be called" (Luke 1:32, 35).

This does not mean that the Qumran text contains a reference to Jesus. It does indicate, however, that some sectarian Jews were already using the title "son of God" to refer to an exalted messiah to come. This passage is further evidence that the Christians who wrote the Gospels drew on imagery and language from earlier Jewish messianic literature.

A COMMUNITY COMMENTARY

A portion of the Habakkuk Commentary (*pesher*) appears here. This text consists of quotes from the Biblical text of Habakkuk along with applicative commentaries. For instance, Habakkuk 1:13 reads, "Why do you look on faithless men and remain silent when the wicked swallows up one more righteous than he?" The Habakkuk Commentary explains: "This refers to the 'house of Absalom' and their cronies who kept silent when charges were leveled against the [Qumran] Teacher [of Righteousness] who was expounding the Law aright, and who did not come to his aid against the Man of Lies when the latter rejected the Torah in the midst of their entire congregation" (lQpHab 13). Although the specific references in this passage may never be known with certainty, the commentary clearly refers to specific individuals, probably the community leader and his adversaries.

A Shared Eschatological Outlook

There is no doubt that the Qumran covenanters and the early Christians shared a similar eschatological outlook. Both must be regarded as "eschatological" communities in the sense that both had a lively expectation that the end of days would come soon and ordered their communal beliefs and practices according to this article of faith. Under this broad heading several points may be distinguished.

Although both groups had messianic expectations, they are different in some respects. The faith of Qumran was that the last days would bring two messiahs: "They shall depart from none of the counsels of the Law to walk in the stubbornness of their hearts, but shall be ruled by the primitive precepts in which the men of the Community were first instructed until there shall come the Prophet and the Messiahs of Aaron and Israel" (Manual of Discipline 9:9–11; see also the Rule of the Congregation). The more prominent messiah is the priestly one: the messiah of Aaron. The second and apparently lower-ranking messiah is the lay one: the messiah of Israel. Precisely what the messiahs would do, other than officiate at the messianic banquet, is not clear; no text says that they would save others or that they would atone for others' sins, as in the case of the Christian Messiah.

The New Testament picture of Jesus is familiar: the Gospel genealogies trace his ancestry through David's line. Jesus, however, is not only the messiah as descendant of David, but also as the son of God and as savior.

Perhaps the Qumran messiah of Israel is also Davidic. But there is no second messiah in the New Testament, as there was at Qumran. While the New Testament has only one messiah, however, it assigns to him the offices filled by the two Qumran messiahs. The New Testament also speaks of Jesus as a priestly messiah. In the Letter to the Hebrews, as we have seen, Jesus is regarded as a priest after the order of Melchizedek; Jesus as high priest presides over a heavenly sanctuary.

Shared Methods of Interpreting the Bible

Another perspective shared by both Qumran covenanters and early Christians was the way that they interpreted Biblical texts—with a strong eschatological consciousness that the end of days was near.

Among the earliest of the scrolls to be discovered and published was the commentary (or *pesher*) on the book of Habakkuk. Karl Elliger published a book about this commentary as early as 1953. He summarized the assumptions underlying this and similar Qumran commentaries (*pesharim*) on Biblical books: the Biblical writers are speaking about the last days, and the last days are now.[37] Based on these presuppositions, the Qumran sectarians interpreted the Biblical texts as referring to themselves and their leaders; the events of their community's history were being foretold in the Biblical texts. For example, Habakkuk 2:1–2 states:

> I will take my stand to watch, and station myself on the tower, and look forth to see what he will say to me, and what I will answer concerning my complaint. And the Lord answered me: "Write the vision; make it plain upon tablets, so he may run who reads it."

The commentary on Habakkuk from Qumran explains these verses as follows: "God told Habakkuk to write down that which would happen to the final generation, but He did not make known to him when time would come to an end. And as for that which He said, 'That he who reads may read it speedily' [= "so he may run who reads it" in Habakkuk 2:2], interpreted, this concerns the Teacher of Righteousness, to whom God made known all the mysteries of the words of His servants the Prophets" (Habakkuk Commentary [also known as 1QpHab] 7:1–5).

Numerous New Testament passages evidence the same eschatological reading of Biblical texts, interpreting them as if they foretold and applied directly to contemporary events. Take the story of Pentecost in Acts 2. In this passage, the apostolic band has been speaking in tongues by virtue of the Holy Spirit that has been poured over them. The local population is perplexed and mocks them. Peter defends those who were speaking in tongues, citing Scripture in support of the linguistic miracle that has just occurred:

> For these men are not drunk, as you suppose, since it is only the third hour of the day; but this is what was spoken by the prophet Joel: "And in the last days [note that Joel does not actually say "in the last days"; he says only "afterward"[38]] it shall be, God declares, that I will pour out my Spirit upon all flesh, and your sons and your daughters shall prophesy, and your young men shall see visions, and your old men shall dream dreams.... (Acts 2:15–17)

Therefore, according to Acts, the prophet Joel proclaimed that the divine Spirit would be poured out in the last days, and that eschatological event actually occurred at the first Christian celebration of Pentecost. This way of interpreting Scripture (Joel in Acts and Habakkuk in the Habakkuk Commentary from Qumran) is identical.

"Tongues as of fire" descend upon the apostles at the first Christian celebration of Pentecost (Acts 2:3–4). Various Biblical commentaries among the Dead Sea Scrolls use scriptural interpretation of Old Testament prophecies as applying to the Qumran sect.

At times the authors of the New Testament and of the Qumran texts rely on the same Biblical text, interpreting it in the same way. We have already seen this in the case of Isaiah 40:3 ("A voice cries out: 'In the wilderness prepare the way of the Lord, make straight in the desert a highway for our God'"). John the Baptist, for the Gospel writers, and the Qumran community, for the Qumran covenanters, are said to be preparing the Lord's way in the wilderness.

Another instance of this is Habakkuk 2:4b: "The righteous live by their faith," one of Paul's favorite prooftexts. He uses it in Galatians 3:11 to support his argument that faith, not works, is the way to become right with God: "Now it is evident that no man is justified before God by the law; for 'He who through faith is righteous shall live'" (see also Romans 1:17).

The Habakkuk Commentary from Qumran offers yet another angle on Habakkuk 2:4b: "This concerns those who observe the Law in the House of Judah, whom God will deliver from the House of Judgment because of their suffering and because of their faith in [or: fidelity to] the Teacher of Righteousness" (Habakkuk Commentary 8:1–3). The same passage that for

The Habakkuk Pesher, or commentary, from Qumran.

Paul dealt with a way of righteousness other than the path of the law was at Qumran a verse that *encouraged* faithfulness to that law and fidelity to the Teacher who expounded it correctly. Yet both use the same text and the same method of interpretation.

Shared Doctrines

The eschatological nature of these two communities can also be seen in some of the major doctrines they embraced. For example, both employ dualistic language to describe the options in the universe: there are just two positions, with no mediating ground between. Since both communities are still Jewish at this time, the dualism is ethical; the two opposing camps (or principles) are light and darkness. One of the best-known passages in the scrolls says:

> He [God] has created man to govern the world, and has appointed for him two spirits in which to walk until the time of His visitation: the spirits of truth and falsehood. Those born of truth spring from a fountain of light, but those born of falsehood spring from a source of darkness. All the children of righteousness are ruled by the ways of light, but all the children of falsehood are ruled by the Angel of Darkness and walk in the ways of darkness. (Manual of Discipline 3:18–21)

Perpetual conflict marks the relation between the two camps:

> For God has established the spirits in equal measure until the final age, and has set everlasting hatred between their divisions. Truth abhors the works of falsehood, and falsehood hates all the ways of truth. And their struggle is fierce in all their arguments, for they do not walk together. (Manual of Discipline 4:16–18)

However, God has "ordained an end for falsehood and at the time of the visitation He will destroy it for ever" (Manual of Discipline 4:18–19). Another Qumran text, the Scroll of the War of the Sons of Light Against the Sons of Darkness, contains an elaborate description of the final battles between the sons of light and the sons of darkness. Though powerful angels will fight on both sides, God will, in his good time, decide the issue in favor of the light.

This language is hardly strange to readers of the New Testament. Similar rhetoric appears in the writings of both Paul (in 2 Corinthians 6:14–7:1) and John.

In John 8:12, the author quotes Jesus as saying: "I am the light of the world; he who follows me will in darkness, but will have the light of life."

As at Qumran, John uses the light/darkness contrast, not in its literal, but in an ethical, sense. As at Qumran, so in John the realms of light and darkness are in conflict: "The light shines in the darkness, and the darkness has not overcome it" (John 1:5). In John 12:35–36, the evangelist tells us: "The light is with you a little longer. Walk while you have the light, lest the darkness overtake you; he who walks in darkness does not know where he goes. While you have the light, believe in the light, that you may be sons of the light" (see also John 3:19–20; 1 John 1:6; 2:9–10). Thus, the followers of Jesus, like the Qumran covenanters, styled themselves "the sons of the light."

The Christian belief about the end is clear. A number of passages speak of Christ's return, the resurrection of the good and the evil, and the ultimate victory of the former under Christ's banner (for example, 1 Corinthians 15:20–28, 51–57). The resurrection of Jesus is a guarantee that those who belong to him will also rise in physical form.

Whether the Qumran covenanters believed in a bodily resurrection is not entirely clear, but they certainly believed in the immortality of the soul. The first-century Jewish historian Josephus tells of Essenes who under torture "cheerfully resigned their souls, confident that they would receive them back again. For it is a fixed belief of theirs that the body is corruptible and its constituent matter impermanent, but that the soul is immortal and imperishable."[39]

The implication from this passage seems to be that, while the Essenes believed in the immortality of the soul, they did not believe in the resurrection of the body, as did the early Christians. The Qumran texts too mention "life without end" (Manual of Discipline 4:7; The Damascus Rule [CD] 3:20, etc.). They may also mention a resurrection of bodies, although this is not absolutely clear.

The difficulty arises because the best available evidence from the published Qumran texts is a poetic passage, and thus its reference to the author's being raised from Sheol (the realm of the dead) to an eternal height may be figurative language for God's delivering him from dire straits to a renewed life rather than a literal bodily resurrection (see Hymns Scroll 3.19–22). However, Hippolytus, an early Christian writer (ca. 170–236) who, like Josephus, describes Essene beliefs, claims that the Essenes did accept the doctrine of the resurrection of bodies.[40]

An as-yet-unpublished Qumran text may now confirm Hippolytus's statement.[41] Emile Puech of the École Biblique in Jerusalem is editing a Hebrew text, inherited from the late Jean Starcky, that Puech dates to the first half of the first century B.C.E. It reads in part: "And they [those who curse] will be for death [while] the One who gives life will [rai]se to life the dead of his people."[42] So the Qumran covenanters may well have believed, as did the early Christians, in a bodily resurrection.

What can we conclude from all this? Clearly, the Qumran literature and the New Testament are similar to one another in numerous and diverse ways.

From the similarities, at least two conclusions can be drawn: (1) the early church grew upon Jewish soil to a far greater extent than previously supposed; and (2) a larger number of the early church's beliefs and practices than previously suspected were not unique to it.

On the other hand, the Qumran scrolls also help to highlight Christianity's uniqueness. This lies not so much in its communal practices and eschatological expectations but in its confession that the son of a carpenter from Nazareth in Galilee was indeed the Messiah and Son of God who taught, healed, suffered, died, rose, ascended, and promised to return someday in glory to judge the living and the dead.

By confessing that their Messiah had come, the Christians also placed themselves further along on the eschatological timetable than the Qumran covenanters, who were still awaiting the arrival of their two messiahs.

As we come to understand more about the Qumran texts, I strongly suspect we will also find that the centrality of Torah, its proper interpretation, and obedience to it figured more prominently in Essene doctrine. This, too, stands in stark contrast with at least

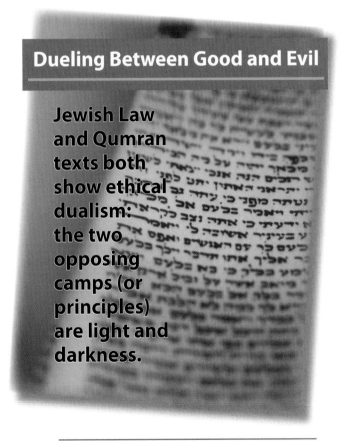

Dueling Between Good and Evil

Jewish Law and Qumran texts both show ethical dualism: the two opposing camps (or principles) are light and darkness.

the Pauline form of Christianity, in which the Mosaic Torah was not to be imposed upon Gentile Christians and justification was obtained through faith, quite apart from observance of the law.

One final note: in light of the significant parallels—and major differences—between the Qumran texts and the New Testament, it is puzzling that the Essenes are never mentioned by name in the New Testament. Some have suggested that they are mentioned but by a different designation (for example, the Herodians[43]). Others have tried to explain their absence on the ground that the groups who are mentioned—the Pharisees and Sadducees—tend to figure in polemical contexts, while the Essenes, with whom Jesus and the first Christians had more in common, do not appear precisely because there were fewer controversies with them or because the Essenes did not debate with outsiders.[44]

A fully satisfying answer escapes us—perhaps because we do not actually know the Semitic term that lies behind the Greek name "Essenes." As this statement implies, the Essenes are not mentioned by that name in rabbinic literature either. Nor, for that matter, does the name Essene appear in the Qumran literature. So we are still left with a few puzzles to figure out.

I wish to thank my colleague Stephen Goranson for reading a draft of this paper and offering helpful comments on it.

NOTES

1. André Dupont-Sommer, *The Dead Sea Scrolls: A Preliminary Survey* (Oxford: Basil Blackwell, 1952), 99 (the preface is dated July 14, 1950). He felt the need to defend these formulations in a later book; see *The Jewish Sect of Qumran and the Essenes: New Studies on the Dead Sea Scrolls* (New York: MacMillan, 1955), 160–62.

2. Later in the same year, Wilson published an expanded version of the article in book form; see *The Scrolls from the Dead Sea* (London: Collins, 1955), 104.

3. Wilson, *The Scrolls from the Dead Sea,* 102.

4. Wilson, *The Scrolls from the Dead Sea,* 104.

5. Wilson, *The Scrolls from the Dead Sea,* 114.

6. Millar Burrows, *The Dead Sea Scrolls* (New York: Viking, 1955).

7. Burrows, *The Dead Sea Scrolls,* 327.

8. Burrows, *The Dead Sea Scrolls,* 328.

9. Burrows, *The Dead Sea Scrolls,* 343.

10. *The Scrolls and the New Testament* (ed. Krister Stendahl; New York: Harper & Row, 1957).

11. Stendahl, "An Introduction and a Perspective," in *The Scrolls and the New Testament,* 16–17.

12. The quotation is from Rudolf Bultmann, *Theology of the New Testament* (2 vols.; New York: Charles Scribner's Sons, 1951–1955), 1:42.

13. Frank M. Cross, *The Ancient Library of Qumran and Modern Biblical Studies* (reprint, Grand Rapids, Mich.: Baker, 1980), 203–4. Mention should also be made of the very brief statement that J. T. Milik devotes to the subject in his *Ten Years of Discovery in the Wilderness of Judaea* (London: SCM, 1959), 142–43. He notes literary, institutional, and doctrinal parallels and argues that Essene influence on the early church increased after the time of Jesus and the first disciples, especially in Jewish Christianity.

14. Herbert Braun, *Qumran und das Neue Testament* (Tübingen: Mohr Siebeck, 1966).

15. See, for example, Geza Vermes, *The Dead Sea Scrolls: Qumran in Perspective* (Philadelphia: Fortress, 1977), 211–21.

16. See, for example, Robert H. Eisenman, *Maccabees, Zadokites, Christians and Qumran: A New Hypothesis of Qumran Origins* (Leiden: Brill, 1983).

17. Barbara Thiering, *Redating the Teacher of Righteousness* (Sydney: Theological Explorations, 1979); and *The Gospels and Qumran: A New Hypothesis* (Sydney: Theological Explorations, 1981).

18. J. L. Teicher, "The Dead Sea Scrolls—Documents of the Jewish-Christian Sect of Ebionites," *Journal of Jewish Studies* 3 (1951): 67–99.

19. Regarding Eisenman, see Michael Baigent and Richard Leigh, *The Dead Sea Scrolls Deception* (London: Jonathan Cape, 1991). Also see Hershel Shanks, "Is the Vatican Suppressing the Dead Sea Scrolls?" *Biblical Archaeology Review* 17.6 (November-December 1991).

20. Translation of Vermes, *The Dead Sea Scrolls in English* (Harmondsworth, U.K.: Penguin, 1962), as are all other quotations from the scrolls, unless otherwise indicated.

21. Cross (*The Ancient Library of Qumran,* 233) notes that the *mbqr* and the *pqyd* (usually translated as *episkopos* in the Greek version of the Hebrew Bible) appear to be the same individual.

22. Joseph Fitzmyer, "The Qumran Scrolls and the New Testament after Forty Years," *Revue de Qumran* 13 (1988): 613–15.

23. For bibliography and discussion of this point, see Braun, *Qumran und das Neue Testament,* 1:201–4. As Fitzmyer has pointed out, 2 Corinthians 6:18 cites 2 Samuel 7:14, a passage that is also quoted in 4QFlorilegium ("4Q Testimonia and the New Testament," *Theological Studies* 18 [1957]: 534–35).

24. Josephus, *Antiquities of the Jews* 15.371. Translation of H. St. J. Thackeray (Loeb Classical Library; Cambridge, Mass.: Harvard University Press).

25. See Kurt Schubert, "The Sermon on the Mount and the Qumran Texts" in Stendahl, *The Scrolls and the New Testament*, 118–28.

26. William H. Brownlee ("John the Baptist in the New Light of Ancient Scrolls" in Stendahl, *The Scrolls and the New Testament,* 33–53) discussed these issues at length and proposed that John may have been raised by the Essenes, who, according to Josephus, adopted the children of others and taught them their principles while they were still young (*Jewish War* 2.120).

27. The texts have been published translated and analyzed by Carol Newsom, *Songs of the Sabbath Sacrifice: A Critical Edition* (Atlanta: Scholars Press, 1985); see her comments on pages 37, 133, and 144. See also Fitzmyer, "The Qumran Scrolls and the New Testament," 618–19. Some caution is in order because Melchizedek's name is never fully preserved in any of the fragmentary remains of these manuscripts.

28. Josephus (*Jewish War* 2.122) and Pliny the Elder (*Natural History* 5.15) also refer to the community property of the Essenes.

29. There is a dittography (unintentional repetition of letters or words while copying) in lines 5–6.

30. Translation of Lawrence Schiffman, *The Eschatological Community of the Dead Sea Scrolls: A Study of the Rule of the Congregation* (Atlanta: Scholars Press, 1989), 53–55.

31. Schiffman, *The Eschatological Community,* 67.

32. An early and important study of this parallel is Karl Georg Kuhn's "The Lord's Supper and the Communal Meal at Qumran" in Stendahl, *The Scrolls and the New Testament,* 65–93.

33. For a brief and precise presentation of the evidence and bibliography for this debate, see Joseph Fitzmyer, *The Dead Sea Scrolls: Major Publications and Tools for Study* (rev. ed.; Atlanta: Scholars Press, 1990), 180–86.

34. Annie Jaubert, *The Date of the Last Supper* (Staten Island, N.Y.: Alba House, 1965).

35. Fitzmyer, "The Qumran Scrolls and the New Testament after Forty Years," *Revue de Qumran* 13 (1988): 617. The text has been given the siglum 4QpsDan [pseudo-Daniel] Aa (4Q246) and dates from the last third of the first century B.C.E. For more detail, see Fitzmyer, "The Contribution of Qumran Aramaic to the Study of the New Testament," in his *A Wandering Aramean: Collected Aramaic Essays* (Missoula, Mont.: Scholars Press: 1979) 90–94 102–7. See also "An Unpublished Dead Sea Scroll Text Parallels Luke's Infancy Narrative," sidebar to "Dead Sea Scroll Variation on 'Show and Tell'—It's Called 'Tell, But No Show,'" *Biblical Archaeology Review* 16.2 (March-April 1990).

36. See Fitzmyer, "The Contribution of Qumran Aramaic," 98.

37. Karl Elliger, *Studien zum Habakuk-Kommentar vom Toten Meer* (Tübingen: Mohr Siebeck, 1953) 150–64. The wording of the assumptions given here is a paraphrase of what he wrote.

38. Joel 2:28 (3:1 in Hebrew).

39. Josephus, *Jewish War* 2.153–154. Josephus also notes their belief in the immortality of the soul in his *Antiquities of the Jews* 18.18.

40. Hippolytus, *Refutation of All Heresies* 9.27, 1.

41. If so, we would conclude that Josephus distorted Essene beliefs, as he does Pharisaic beliefs about the resurrection, in order to appeal to the tastes of his larger, Greek-reading audience, to whom it may have seemed peculiar.

42. Emile Puech, "Les Esséniens et la vie future," *Le Monde de la Bible* 4 (1978): 38–40: The quotation is my translation of his French rendering (p. 40). The text in question is apparently 4Q521.

43. Josephus reports that Herod favored the Essenes (*Antiquities of the Jews* 15.372). See Yigael Yadin, "The Temple Scroll—The Longest and Most Recently Discovered Dead Sea Scroll," *Biblical Archaeology Review* 10.5 (September-October 1984).

44. See the discussion in Geza Vermes, *The Dead Sea Scrolls: Qumran in Perspective* (Philadelphia: Fortress, 1977), 220.

A SADDUCEAN SETTLEMENT?

The Qumran ruins stand on the desolate slopes of the Judean wilderness, overlooking the shore of the Dead Sea. Near the tip of the ridge across the ravine from the settlement, the caves where the Dead Sea Scrolls were found penetrate the cliffs.

For decades Qumran has been generally regarded as the remains of a community of Essenes. However, Lawrence Schiffman believes that the Qumran sect may have been Sadducean in origin.

SIGNIFICANCE OF THE SCROLLS

A New Perspective on the Texts from the Qumran Caves

By Lawrence H. Schiffman

Dead Sea Scroll scholarship is undergoing a virtual revolution. New ideas and perspectives are percolating among the small group of scholars who dedicate themselves to primary research on the content of the scrolls. Recent publications focus on major changes in the way Dead Sea Scroll research affects our understanding of the history of Judaism and Christianity. What are these new perspectives? How do they differ from the scroll scholarship of the past? What is likely to emerge from recently published materials? These are the questions we will try to explore here.

In a strange way, Dead Sea Scroll research really began fifty years before the first Dead Sea Scrolls were discovered in 1947. In 1896, a Cambridge University scholar named Solomon Schechter traveled to Egypt to purchase the remains of the Cairo Genizah, a vast treasure-trove of Hebrew manuscripts from the storehouse of a synagogue in Fustat, Old Cairo. Among the many important documents he recovered were two medieval manuscripts of part of a hitherto unknown work now known to scholars as the Damascus Document (because it mentions an exile to Damascus).

Schechter immediately realized that these manuscripts represented the texts of an ancient Jewish sect far older than the medieval copies in the Cairo Genizah. Another scholar, Louis Ginzberg, in a later series of articles on the Damascus Document,[1] was able to outline the nature of this sect—which turned out to be the Dead Sea Scroll sect. Ginzberg realized that the Damascus Document found in the Cairo Genizah was the remnant of a sect of Jews that had separated from the dominant patterns of Second Temple Judaism before the Roman destruction of the temple in 70 C.E. Ginzberg was able to describe the laws, the theology, and even aspects of the history of this sect. We now know that Ginzberg missed the mark only in regard to his emphasis on the closeness of these sectarians to Pharisaism.

In 1947 in a cave in the cliffs near Wadi Qumran, overlooking the Dead Sea just south of Jericho, a shepherd came upon the first of the documents now known collectively as the Dead Sea Scrolls. Seven scrolls were eventually sold, in two lots, to the Hebrew University and the state of Israel, and they are now housed in the Shrine of the Book of the Israel Museum.

THE SCROLLERY'S SCRIBES

This long room at the Rockefeller Museum was set aside for the storage and study of scroll fragments. Dubbed "the Scrollery," with long tables and huddled scholars, the room looks like a large-scale scriptorium. Some of the scrolls written by ancient scholar-scribes at Qumran are almost certainly among the fragments that cover these tables and fill the storage drawers.

A s the British mandate over Palestine drew to a close, and the state of Israel was proclaimed in 1948, action shifted to the kingdom of Jordan, which in the aftermath of Israel's War of Independence held the rocky area where the first scrolls had been found. In the early 1950s the Bedouin—and, to a much lesser extent, professional archaeologists—uncovered enormous numbers of additional fragments and some complete scrolls in ten other caves. Particularly rich was a site known as Cave 4, in which an estimated 15,000 fragments—parts of nearly six hundred different scrolls—were discovered. All of these texts were collected at the Rockefeller Museum in East Jerusalem, then under Jordanian control.

The manuscripts were carefully sorted by a team of scholars assembled primarily from the American Schools of Oriental Research and the École Biblique. The initial achievements of this group were remarkable: they assembled the fragments into larger columns, stored in "plates"; they transcribed the texts; they even prepared a concordance of all the words in the non-Biblical texts. It was only later, in the early 1960s, when funds ran out and other factors, both personal and political, intervened, that work came to a virtual standstill for almost twenty years.

The texts in Israel's hands were promptly published. Indeed, three of the scrolls had already been published by the American Schools of Oriental Research before Israeli acquisition. The other four scrolls in Israeli hands were published by Israeli scholars E. L. Sukenik, Nahman Avigad, and Yigael Yadin.

After the Six-Day War in 1967, the Israelis acquired the last of the nearly complete scrolls (as opposed to fragmentary texts), the lengthy Temple Scroll. The crown of Israeli scroll achievement was Yigael Yadin's publication of this important text.

Yadin's Hebrew publication of the Temple Scroll in 1977 sparked renewed interest in the field. At about the same time, significant publications from the original Jordanian lot began to appear. Especially important were fragments from the *Book of Enoch* published by J. T. Milik and liturgical texts published by Maurice Baillet. Complaints about the slow pace of publication also brought considerable pressure on scholars to speed up the process. Eventually, a significantly expanded team of scholars succeeded in publishing critical editions of all of the Qumran texts.

While the first generation of Dead Sea Scroll scholars consisted primarily of specialists in the Hebrew Bible and the New Testament, the scholars now involved in research on the scrolls are, to a large extent, a new generation. These researchers are undertaking the study of particularly Jewish issues in the scrolls: Jewish history, law, theology, and messianism. It is to this generation that I belong, having been occupied almost full-time for decades in Dead Sea Scroll research (Qumran studies, as it is known in the trade). Not being bound to the original theories of those who first identified the authors of the scrolls, this younger generation of scholars has opened anew all kinds of questions pertaining to the origins of the texts.

Dating the Scrolls

The initial battle of the Dead Sea Scrolls involved their date and the identity of the people who wrote them. One group of scholars, collected around Solomon Zeitlin of Dropsie College in Philadelphia, argued that they were medieval documents associated with the Karaites, a Jewish sect that based its laws and customs solely on the Bible and rejected the Talmud.[2]

Another group of scholars argued for a late first-century C.E. date. They connected the scrolls either with the Zealots (militant Jewish rebels in the First Jewish Revolt against Rome, which culminated in the destruction of Jerusalem in 70 C.E.) or with early Christians.

These theories all ultimately failed, resulting in a virtual scholarly consensus that the scrolls are to be

This text is written in paleo- (or "old") Hebrew. Note that the letters are less squared off and include more diagonal strokes and fewer verticals than in the later "square Hebrew." Paleo-Hebrew script is a variant of Phoenician script and was used in the First Temple period. Although we have no examples of biblical writings earlier than the Dead Sea Scrolls, we know that the earliest copies of the books of the Torah and the early prophets were written in paleo-Hebrew.

The practice of writing sacred texts in paleo-Hebrew centuries after it had gone out of style was undoubtedly an expression of archaizing reverence, akin in spirit to the modern practice of reading the Torah in Hebrew during synagogue worship, even though it is studied and discussed in the modern language of the congregation.

By contrast, some Qumran texts were written in Aramaic, the spoken language of the Jews in Palestine during the last centuries of the Second Temple period (second century B.C.E. to first century C.E.).

dated primarily to the Hasmonean period (152–63 B.C.E.) and the Early Roman period (63 B.C.E.–68 C.E). Indeed, some material from the Qumran caves is even earlier. This dating is supported by archaeological evidence from the Qumran settlement adjacent to the caves where the scrolls were found, by carbon-14 tests of the cloth in which the scrolls were wrapped in ancient times, by paleographic evidence (the shape and stance of the letters), and, more generally, by the content of the scrolls then published.

Were They Essene Documents?

As a consensus on the dating of the scrolls developed, so did a consensus on the identity of the sect with which the scrolls were to be associated: the Essenes. The Essenes were a group or sect of Jews who lived a strictly regulated life of piety and who shared property in common. While their center was located at the Dead Sea, the group was said to have had members spread throughout the cities of Palestine

as well. The Essenes are described by the first-century Jewish historian Josephus; by his Alexandrian Jewish contemporary, the philosopher Philo; and by the first-century Roman historian Pliny. That the Qumran texts were associated with the Essenes was first suggested by E. L. Sukenik, then elaborated in the works of Frank M. Cross, Millar Burrows and André Dupont-Sommer. The Essene hypothesis quickly became, and still remains, the reigning theory.

The theory has a certain surface attractiveness. Josephus, Philo, and Pliny all describe Essenes on the shore of the Dead Sea, living in a manner not inconsistent with what the remains at the Qumran settlement seemed to reveal. (The excavations were conducted in the mid-1950s. Unfortunately, the director of the excavation, Roland de Vaux of the École Biblique, never succeeded in publishing a final excavation report; only preliminary reports and a survey volume appeared.[3]) Furthermore, in many ways what was known about the Essenes paralleled what was found, or seemed to be implied, in the Qumran texts: initiation rites, organizational patterns, a special calendar. The Essenes were therefore assumed to be the authors of virtually all of the scrolls, except the Biblical texts and copies of some previously known apocryphal works such as *Jubilees*.

The Essene theory also had another dimension: many doctrines of the Essenes, then taken to be synonymous with the Qumran sect, had parallels in early Christianity. The Essenes thus became a kind of precursor to Christianity, perhaps even a harbinger.

Many devout Jews came to the Judean wilderness, initially to escape the corruption of the royal and religious leadership of the Hasmonean kingdom in Jerusalem, later to distance themselves from the extravagant decadence during the Herodian era and the contaminating presence of Romans and other foreigners. Why were pious Jews drawn to this region in particular? Perhaps it was a combination of the prophetic visions of spiritual renewal in the wilderness and the isolation of the Judean wilderness from the world of Jerusalem.

Methodologically, the identification of the Essenes with the Qumran sect was often supported with a circular argument. If the sectarian materials in the Dead Sea texts could be linked to the Essenes, then all information in the Greek sources (Philo, Josephus, and Pliny) could be read into and harmonized with the evidence of the scrolls. And if the scrolls were Essene, then they could in turn be used to interpret the material in Philo, Josephus, and Pliny. A similar circularity was used to connect the scrolls with New Testament texts. Material from the New Testament regarding the early church was read back into the scrolls and vice versa. This approach, the dominant hypothesis for some forty years, yielded the "monks," "monastery," "bishop," "celibacy," and numerous other terminological exaggerations used to describe Qumran texts, behind which lay a distinct set of preconceptions. For the most part, the fallacy of these arguments somehow escaped scholarly scrutiny.

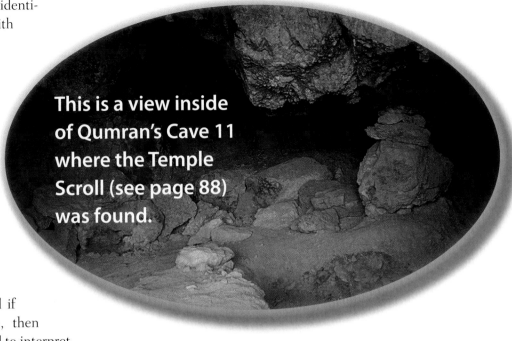

This is a view inside of Qumran's Cave 11 where the Temple Scroll (see page 88) was found.

Beginning in 1985 with a conference held at New York University[4] and continuing to the present, contradictions of the "official" Essene hypothesis were voiced as the field of learning advanced. Gradually a new nonconsensus began to emerge. Indeed, it is now understood that the term "Essene" may have designated a variety of sectarian groups that had certain common characteristics. Accordingly, most scholars now refer to the "Qumran sect," no longer assuming that it is the Essenes. And the character of the "ancient library" is being reevaluated.

A Variety of Texts

The collection of Qumran texts consists of Biblical manuscripts, the sect's special texts (generally written according to the linguistic peculiarities of the sect), plus a whole variety of other texts collected by the people who lived at Qumran. The relationship of these other texts to the sect is unclear. Many texts were apparently brought to Qumran from elsewhere and held because they had some affinities with the beliefs of the sectarians. These texts may have emerged from earlier, somewhat different sectarian circles, or perhaps they came from contemporary groups close in their ideology to the Qumran sect. These texts cannot be regarded as representing the Qumran sect itself because they do not include its characteristic themes, polemics, and terminology, nor are they written in the distinctive language and style of the works of the sect.

Recently several fragmentary texts were published from Masada (Herod's wilderness fortress about 35 miles south of Qumran), which was occupied by rebels during the First Jewish Revolt against Rome. In addition, a manuscript of the Sabbath Songs, known in several manuscripts from Qumran, was found at Masada. Thus, the Jewish defenders of Masada possessed books of the same kind as those found in the Qumran collection but that were not directly associated with the sect itself. In other words, many of the works found at Qumran were the common heritage of Second Temple Judaism and did not originate in, and were not confined to, Qumran sectarian circles.

The sectarian documents of the Qumran sect, however, form the core of this varied collection. What was the sect, and what was its origin? A text known in scholarly circles as MMT (for *Miqsat Ma'aseh ha-Torah*—literally, "Some Rulings Pertaining to the Torah"—abbreviated 4QMMT, 4Q referring to Cave 4 at Qumran) is likely to shed considerable new light on these questions. Known also as the Halakhic Letter, referring to the fact that it appears to be a letter and contains about twenty-two religious laws (*halakhot*), MMT is essentially a foundation document of the Qumran sect. Although it was discovered in 1952, its contents were made known only in 1984. The ancient author of MMT asserts that the sect broke away from the Jewish establishment in Jerusalem because of differences involving these religious laws. He asserts that the sect will return if their opponents, who are pictured as knowing that the sectarians are right all along, will recant.

I have compared the laws in MMT with passages in the rabbinic texts known as the Mishnah and the Talmud, which identify the legal views of the Phari-

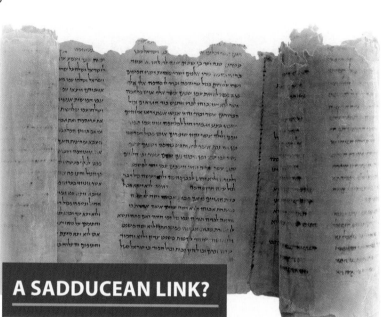

A SADDUCEAN LINK?

The Temple Scroll, found in Cave 11 (previous page) at Qumran, is about 27 feet long, making it the longest of the Dead Sea Scrolls. Although the scroll itself dates to about the last part of the first century B.C.E., the text of which it is a copy probably reached its final form in the Hasmonean period (152–63 B.C.E.), soon after the appearance of the Qumran sect. The author/editor of the Temple Scroll apparently used Sadducean sources from before the Hasmonean period, for some of the laws in the scroll's text parallel Sadducean laws found in MMT or known from rabbinic literature. In some cases, however, the Temple Scroll gives a scriptural basis for a law, whereas MMT cites just the law. This difference provides an insight into the viewpoint of the early Sadducees, who required their laws to be based on scripture.

sees and the Sadducees, two Jewish movements that flourished before the Roman destruction of the temple. From this investigation I have been able to show that the origins of the Qumran sect are Sadducean. The Jewish sect of the Sadducees, best known as the opponents of the Pharisees, broke away from their fellow Jews after the Maccabean revolt (168–164 B.C.E.), in which the Hasmonean Jewish rulers regained control of their land and temple from the Seleucid Syrian overlord Antiochus IV. The Hasmoneans took control of the temple, making common cause with the Pharisees. This situation lasted until the Herodian period, which began with the assumption of power by Herod the Great in 37 B.C.E. Some of the Sadducees bent their principles and adjusted to the new situation. Others did not. For those who were unwilling to adjust to the new reality or to compromise their deeply held legal and exegetical principles, this situation proved intolerable. Although quite technical, the religious laws of the two groups differed very considerably. It is in this context that we must understand MMT.

MMT, which dates to the Hasmonean period, is a letter sent by those unwilling to accept the legal rulings enunciated by the Hasmonean high priests. In its legal sections, MMT argues with those compromising Sadducees, setting forth, on the one hand, what the correct law is and, on the other hand, what the law enunciated by the Hasmoneans is. At the end of the letter, the author addresses the Hasmonean ruler himself and attempts to sway him to MMT's views by warning him that God blesses only those rulers who follow God's ways.[5]

The MMT revolutionizes the question of Qumran origins and requires us to reconsider the entire Essene hypothesis. It shows beyond question that either the sect was not Essene, but was Sadducean, or that the Essene movement must be totally redefined as having emerged out of Sadducean beginnings. Such a possibility is in agreement with the basic conclusions of Schechter, reached only on the basis of the Damascus Document before the discovery of the Dead Sea Scrolls. Schechter entitled this text a Zadokite Work and outlined its Sadducean connections.

In my opinion, the most likely scenario, based on the entire collection of Qumran documents published thus far, but drawing especially on MMT, is that a process of sectarianism and separatist mentality grew throughout the Hasmonean period and blossomed during the Herodian period. As a result, a group of originally Sadducean priests, under the leadership of the Teacher of Righteousness (who, in my view, came to lead the sect only after MMT was written), developed into the group that left us the sectarian texts found at Qumran.

Varied Judaisms

As more and more scrolls are published, our understanding of the nature of the collection widens. It is now becoming increasingly clear that the scrolls are the primary source for the study of Judaism in all its varieties in the last centuries before the Common Era. In short, this corpus does not simply give us an entry into the sect that inhabited the nearby settlement, but it also has an enormous amount to tell us about the widely varying Judaisms of the Hasmonean and Herodian periods. In assessing the importance of the collection, we must remember that almost no other primary Hebrew or Aramaic sources exist for the reconstruction of Judaism during these periods. Thus these documents provide a critical background for the study of the later emergence both of rabbinic Judaism and of the early Christian church.

Scholars used to think that the library was entirely the product of the inhabitants of Qumran. Instead, it can now be stated that this hoard of manuscripts includes material representing a variety of Jewish groups as well as polemics against other Jewish groups. As a result of this new understanding, much more can be done with the scrolls.

Specifically, it was believed until recently that we have no contemporary sources for the Pharisees during the Hasmonean period. Because the Pharisees

JOSEPHUS ON THE ESSENES

"For there are three philosophical sects among the Jews. The followers of the first of whom are the Pharisees; of the second the Sadducees; and the third sect, who pretends to a severer discipline, and called Essenes. These last are Jews by birth, and seem to have a greater affection for one another than the other sects have. These Essenes reject pleasures as an evil, but esteem continence, and the conquest over our passions, to be virtue. They neglect wedlock, but choose out other persons' children, while they are pliable, and fit for learning; and esteem them to be of their kindred, and form them according to their own manners." (*Jewish War* 8.2)

THE DEAD SEA SCROLLS 89

bequeathed their approach to the rabbinic Judaism that emerged after the Roman destruction of Jerusalem, this lack of sources was particularly keenly felt. The situation was much the same with the Sadducees. Nor could we make much sense of the various apocalyptic groups whose existence scholars could only assume.

In the last few years, however, we have come to realize that this evaluation is incorrect. The scrolls inform us not only about the unusual sect that inhabited the ruins of Qumran but also about the other groups as well.

Let us begin with the Pharisees. This elusive group of lay teachers and expounders of the Torah—previously known only from later accounts in Josephus, the largely polemical treatment in the New Testament, and the scattered references in talmudic literature—is now coming to life before our eyes. So far as we can tell from the published material, the scrolls include material on the Pharisees only in polemical contexts, but this can still tell us a great deal.

The polemics against the Pharisees are of two kinds. In the better-known, sectarian texts, the Pharisees are called by various code words, such as "Ephraim."[6] In these texts, the Pharisees are said to be the "builders of the wall"[7]; that is, they built fences around the Torah by legislating additional regulations designed to ensure its observance. These fences were no more acceptable to the Qumran sect than the *halakhot* (laws) of the Pharisees. The sect, using a play on words, derisively called the Pharisees *doreshe ḥalaqot*, best translated as "those who expound false laws."[8] The same text refers to the *talmud* (literally, "study") of "Ephraim" as falsehood, no doubt a reference to the Pharisaic method of deriving new, extended laws from expressions of Scripture. In these texts from Qumran, we see that Josephus's description of the Pharisees and their traditions—which were the precursor of the concept of oral rabbinic law that became embodied in the Talmud—were already in place in the Hasmonean period.

A second type of anti-Pharisaic polemic is reflected in MMT. In MMT, the author castigates his opponents and then expresses his own view, specifying the legal violation in the opponents' views. In a number of cases, the laws the author(s) of MMT opposes are the same laws that later rabbinic sources

TWICE BURIED . . .

The 10th-century C.E. manuscript shown here provided a first glimpse of an ancient Jewish sect. Discovered in 1897 in the storeroom of a Cairo synagogue by the Jewish scholar Solomon Schechter and then named the Zadokite Fragments (now known as the Damascus Document), this text furiously condemns the ritual practices of the sect's opponents. From the language and ideas contained within it, Schechter concluded that his find was a medieval version of a much earlier text.

attribute to the Pharisees, and the laws the author(s) of MMT espouse match those of the Sadducees as reflected in later rabbinic texts. Accordingly, we now have good reason to believe that in MMT we have *halakhot*, as they were already called in the Hasmonean period, maintained by the Pharisees.

When the Dead Sea Scrolls were discovered, several copies of the Damascus Document (shown here) were among the finds. While this and the other scrolls tell us much about the Dead Sea Scroll sect, they also broaden our knowledge of other ancient Jewish groups. In particular, the views of the rabbis of the Talmud are turning out to be remarkably consistent with those of the Pharisees, who came to prominence in the mid-second century B.C.E.

This letter requires that the view of prominent scholars—most notably Jacob Neusner—who doubted the reliability of the rabbis regarding the Pharisees must be reevaluated. The talmudic materials are far more accurate than previously thought. This is true in at least two respects.

First, the Pharisaic view did indeed predominate during much of the Hasmonean period. In short, this is not a later talmudic anachronistic invention. Second, the terminology, and even some of the very laws as recorded in rabbinic sources (some in the name of the Pharisees and others attributed to anonymous first-century sages), were actually used and espoused by the Pharisees. In other words—and this is extremely important—rabbinic Judaism as embodied in the Talmud is not a postdestruction invention, as some scholars had maintained; on the contrary, the roots of rabbinic Judaism reach back at least to the Hasmonean period.

Sadducees, Aristocratic Literalists

The Qumran texts also teach us a great deal about the Sadducees. In the Pesher Nahum they are termed "Menasseh,"[9] the opponents of "Ephraim" (the code word for the Pharisees). Here the Sadducees are described as aristocratic members of the ruling class. This fits the period at the end of Hasmonean rule, just before the Roman conquest of Palestine in 63 B.C.E., when the Pharisees had fallen out with the Hasmoneans. All this accords perfectly with the description of the Sadducees by Josephus. As with the Pharisees, so with the Sadducees: Josephus's description is generally accurate. Moreover, as previously noted, the twenty-two examples of Sadducean laws in MMT frequently match views attributed to the Sadducees in talmudic sources.

A number of Sadducean laws found in MMT also have parallels in the Temple Scroll. In some cases the Temple Scroll provides a scriptural basis when MMT cites only the law. Although the final text of the Temple Scroll was edited in the Hasmonean period, some of its sources were apparently earlier—before the emergence of the Qumran sect, to a time when these teachings were indeed Sadducean. The author/editor of the final text of the complete Temple Scroll, whether a member of the Qumran sect or of some related or similar group, used these Sadducean sources. In recovering the sources of the Temple Scroll, we get a clearer and clearer picture of the views of the Sadducees. We are finally beginning to understand their brand of literalism—barely suggested by the later references in ancient literature that had previously been known. In short, the Sadducees required that all laws be based on Scripture: they rejected laws unrelated to the Bible.

Apocalyptic Jewish Sects

The Qumran scrolls also tell us about various apocalyptic groups whose teachings are so important for our understanding of the later development of aspects of Jewish mysticism as well as Christian apocalypticism.

For these apocalyptic groups, we unfortunately lack all social and historical context—at least so far. Texts like the *Book of Noah,* as well as the books of Daniel and *Enoch,* have a common structure: heavenly secrets of the present and of the end of days are revealed to the hero. These texts often involve heavenly ascents and other journeys of this kind frequently found in later Jewish mysticism. Their notions of immediate messianic fulfillment must have greatly influenced Christian messianism. This influence can also be seen in the messianic pressures for armed Jewish resistance against Roman rule that were important factors in fueling the two Jewish revolts, the First Revolt of 66–70 C.E. and the Second Revolt, the so-called Bar-Kokhba revolt, of 132–135 C.E., both of which had messianic overtones.

At this point I should perhaps comment briefly on the Dead Sea Scroll hypothesis recently put forward by Professor Norman Golb of the University of Chicago. According to him, the Qumran scrolls are from the library of the Jerusalem temple, brought from Jerusalem and hidden at Qumran during the First Jewish Revolt against Rome. The Qumran documents, Golb argues, therefore represent a balanced picture of the Judaism of the Second Temple period. Indeed, he goes so far as to claim that there was no Qumran sect; rather, the settlement at Qumran was, he maintains, a military fortress. In his view, the ruins of Qumran have no relation to the scrolls found in the adjacent caves.[10]

The cemetery of the Qumran community (at left) was on the terrace surface east of the buildings and separated from the settlement by a low wall (not visible in this photo). Excavators counted more than 1,100 graves marked by clusters of stones over the rectangular trenches.

Norman Golb, of the University of Chicago, has theorized that the buildings at Qumran (above) constituted a fortress, rather than a religious retreat. As evidence, he notes that this tower base might indicate that the site was fortified.

Despite the aggressive way in which he has argued for this theory, he has never supported it by a study of, or citations to, the texts themselves. Indeed, he ignores the evidence we have cited from MMT (although, in fairness, at best only a pirated copy of the unpublished texts of MMT was available to him). Equally important, he has also ignored the clear sectarian emphasis of the collection as a whole insofar as it has been published.

Moreover, the settlement at Qumran was constructed in much too unsturdy a manner to be a fortress. Its water supply was completely open and unprotected, contrary to what we would expect of a fortress. Its location was exposed, with its back and one flank abutting a cliff from which it could be attacked and overwhelmed. The wall that surrounded at least part of the settlement was not the wall of a fortress, but a mere enclosure wall, barely thicker than the walls of the buildings inside. Golb relies on the fact that a building at the site was identified by the excavator as a tower. The only reason this building appears to be a tower is because by coincidence it is the only building preserved to the height of its second story. Golb also calls our attention to the fact that graves of women and children, as well as of men, have been found at the site. He correctly argues that this disproves the claim that the site was the monastery of celibate monks. But these graves of women and children also fly in the face of his argument that Qumran was a fortress. In sum, Golb's hypothesis is not valid. It is put forward despite incontrovertible facts, not in an effort to explain doubtful matters on the basis of known information.

Christian Roots in Sectarian Judaism

Let us turn now to what the Qumran texts can teach us about early Christianity. It is clear that many expressions, motifs, and concepts found in early Christianity have their background in sectarian Judaism of the Second Temple period, as reflected in the Qumran texts. This has long been observed. I also agree that the use of postdestruction rabbinic literature, which once served as the primary source for establishing and interpreting the background of Christian ideas, turns out to be misguided in light of our current knowledge of the varied character of Judaism in the Greco-Roman period. Such ideas as the dualism of light and darkness, the presentation of the figure of the messiah as

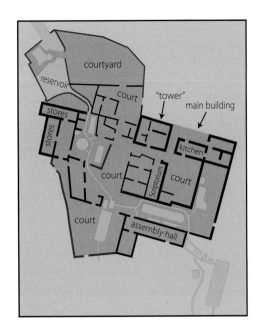

Plan of the Qumran Community

combining a variety of leadership roles known from earlier Hebrew sources, the immediate messianism— all these are ideas we can and do trace in the Qumran texts.

Yet the quest for parallels to, and antecedents of, Christian doctrines and ideas should remain secondary. The better way to use the Qumran texts for understanding early Christianity is to understand them as illuminating the full spectrum of Jewish groups in Hellenistic Palestine. When we compensate for the sectarian emphasis of the collection as a whole, it turns out that the contribution the Qumran texts can make to the prehistory of Christianity is even greater.

Second Temple Judaism can now be seen as a transition period in which the sectarianism and apocalypticism of the period gradually gave way to rabbinic Judaism, on the one hand, and Christianity, on the other. Indeed, it is now clear that the Second Temple period was a kind of sorting-out process.

Until the Maccabean revolt (168–164 B.C.E.), the Jewish communities in Palestine and in the Diaspora fiercely debated the extent to which they would partake of and absorb the Hellenistic culture all around them. The successful Maccabean revolt resolved this issue: extreme Hellenism was over-whelmingly rejected in Palestinian Judaism. While Judaism would therefore not become simply one of the Hellenistic cults, the new cultural environment caused by the contact with

Hellenism led nonetheless to a reevaluation of many issues in Judaism. The variety of responses that developed brought about the splitting of the Jewish community into various groups or, perhaps in some cases, sects, each seeking to dominate the religious scene. The writings of some of these groups and considerable information about others can be gleaned, as we have seen, from the Dead Sea Scrolls.

The competing groups vied with one another throughout the Hasmonean period. This debate finally was resolved only in the aftermath of the Bar-Kokhba revolt (135 C.E.). Apocalyptic messianic tendencies, now much better understood from the sectarian texts from Qumran (and from some of the other preserved there as well), became more and more pronounced among some groups. This led eventually to the two Jewish revolts against Rome. These same trends also led a small group of Jews to conclude that their leader, one Jesus of Nazareth, was indeed the "son of man," interpreted by some as a messianic designation. This term is well known from the book Daniel and also from Enochic texts preserved at Qumran.

Postdestruction rabbinic Judaism based itself, for the most part, on Pharisaism, although it also included aspects of the traditions of the sectarian and apocalyptic groups. Christianity, on the other hand, primarily inherited the immediate apocalypticism of these groups. Christianity also adopted, or adapted, certain dualistic tendencies and a wide variety of motifs found in the doctrines of these groups. In other words, Christianity is to a great extent the continuation of trends within Second Temple Judaism that were rejected by the emerging Pharisaic-rabbinic mainstream.

In Search of the Earliest Biblical Texts

Finally, let us look at the Qumran texts for the light they can shed on the history of the Biblical texts. Here again, recent study requires the modification of earlier held views. In the early years of Qumran studies, it was thought that the Biblical texts found in the cave (at least fragments of every book of the Hebrew Bible except Esther and Song of Songs were found) would somehow illuminate the "original" text that emerged from ancient Israel. This entire notion has been proven wrong. We now know that the transmission of the text in the post-Biblical period resulted in many textual variants. These variants resulted not only from the copying process itself but also from interpretation of the text and linguistic updating, phenomena that could not have been understood before the discovery of the scrolls.[11]

This lavishly decorated Torah scroll contains a version of the five books of Moses known as the Samaritan Pentateuch. Some of the textual variants found in the Samaritan Pentateuch match readings found in other ancient Biblical manuscripts, such as the Septuagint and the texts from Qumran.

Very early in the study of the Biblical manuscripts from Qumran, a theory was put forward, first by William F. Albright[12] and then more fully by Frank M. Cross,[13] that supposedly identified three text types. One of these text types stood behind the Masoretic Text, the traditional Jewish Hebrew text adopted by rabbinic Judaism as authoritative; another text type stood behind the Samaritan Pentateuch (before the introduction of certain Samaritan polemical changes); a third text type stood behind the text preserved only in the Greek translation known as the Septuagint. These three textual families were shown to have co-existed at Qumran, and it was widely assumed that they were represented in roughly equivalent numbers of texts, although this assumption was in fact based only on a limited sample.

Recent studies require a modification of this approach. In fact, most of the Biblical manuscripts at Qumran indicate that the proto-Masoretic text type in fact predominated. Thus, the process of standardiza-

> **The discoveries at Qumran have led scholars to new insights about the development of the texts of the Hebrew Bible.**

tion whereby this text became authoritative in rabbinic Judaism may have taken place much earlier than was previously presumed. In short, the proto-Masoretic tradition was in ascendence by the Hasmonean period. It is likely that this text type was the most common because it was the most ancient. The process of standardization was in reality one of eliminating variant texts. This, indeed, is the picture presented in rabbinic literature.

Another modification of Cross's analysis is also required. Most Biblical texts at Qumran represent, to some extent, mixtures of text types. The Biblical manuscripts commonly share readings with other texts to such an extent that few can be understood as representative purely of a single text type.[14] Indeed, the very notion of text types to a certain extent projects backward in time the textual "witnesses" that have survived in later copies—that is, the Masoretic Hebrew text, the Samaritan Pentateuch, and the Greek Septuagint—which were known to us before the Qumran finds. Had we not had the Septuagint and the Samaritan Bibles, we would never have concluded from the Qumran material itself that three text families existed. A more accurate picture would describe trends reflected in varying degrees in different Biblical texts from Qumran. This would explain much better the predominance of the many mixed texts of the Hebrew Bible found at Qumran.

The claim that New Testament manuscripts were found at Qumran can be dealt with in a sentence. None was found—for a very good reason: New Testament texts are later than the Qumran texts.

What we have described here as to the Qumran collection and its implications is based on wide variety of texts, including MMT, which many earlier scholars were unable to consult. Now that the entire Qumran corpus has been published, students of the varieties of Sec-

ond Temple Judaism and their relevance to rabbinic Judaism and early Christianity have a veritable feast set before them, a feast that will no doubt continue to lead to new insights and further refinements of our understanding of the ancient inhabitants of Qumran and their relation to the various groups with Second Temple Judaism and early Christianity.

NOTES

1. For the full publication of his study, see *An Unknown Jewish Sect* (New York: Jewish Theological Seminary, 1976).

2. Solomon Zeitlin, *The Zadokite Fragments* (Philadelphia: Dropsie College, 1952).

3. The site was excavated in 1953–1956. The survey volume was first published in French in 1961 and then revised as Roland de Vaux, *Archaeology and the Dead Sea Scrolls* (London: Oxford University Press, 1973).

4. See Lawrence H. Schiffman, ed., *Archaeology and History in the Dead Sea Scrolls* (Sheffield: Sheffield Academic Press, 1990). Subsequent conferences were held at London and Manchester (England), Mogilany (Poland), Israel, Groningen (the Netherlands) and again at Mogilany, all of which have generated volumes of the papers presented.

5. See, among others, my essay entitled "The Temple Scroll and the Systems of Jewish Law in the Second Temple Period," in *Temple Scroll Studies* (ed. George J. Brooke; Sheffield: JSOT Press, 1989), 239–55.

6. Pesher Nahum 3–4 i 12; ii 2, 8; iii 5; Pesher Psalms (A) 1–2 ii 17.

7. Damascus Document 4:19, 8:12, 19:25, 31.

8. Hodayot 2:15, 32; Pesher Nahum 3–4 i 2, 7; ii 2, 4; iii 3, 7; Damascus Document 1:18.

9. Pesher Nahum 3–4 iii 9; iv 1, 3, 6; Pesher Psalms (A) 1–2 ii 17.

10. Norman Golb, "The Dead Sea Scrolls, A New Perspective," *The American Scholar* (Spring 1989): 177–207.

11. See Shemaryahu Talmon, *The World of Qumran from Within* (Jerusalem: Magnes; Leiden: Brill, 1989), 71–141.

12. William F. Albright, "New Light on Early Recensions of the Hebrew Bible," *Bulletin of American Schools of Oriental Research* 140 (1955): 27–33.

13. Cross, "The History of the Biblical Text in Light of Discoveries in the Judaean Desert," *Harvard Theological Review* 57 (1964): 281–99.

14. See Emanuel Tov, "A Modern Textual Outlook Based on the Qumran Scrolls," *Hebrew Union College Annual* 53 (1982): 11–27; "Hebrew Biblical Manuscripts from the Judaean Desert: Their Contribution to Textual Criticism," *Journal of Jewish Studies* 39 (1988): 5–37.

credits

PUBLICATION CREDITS

Chapter 1, "How the Dead Sea Scrolls Were Found," was originally published in *Biblical Archaeology Review* 1/4, December 1975.

Chapter 2, "More Scrolls Lie Buried! Recollections from Years Gone By," was originally published as "Recollections from 40 Years Ago: More Scrolls Lie Buried," in *Biblical Archaeology Review* 19/1, January-February 1993.

Chapter 3, "The Dead Sea Scrolls and the People Who Wrote Them," was originally published in *Biblical Archaeology Review* 3/1, March 1977.

Chapter 4, "Publishing the Scrolls: Reflections on Thirty Years of Scholarly Work," was originally published as "Expanded Team of Editors Hard at Work on Variety of Texts," in *Biblical Archaeology Review* 18/4, July-August 1992.

Chapter 5, "The Fluid Bible: The Blurry Line between Biblical and Nonbiblical Texts," was originally published in *Bible Review* 15/3, June 1999.

Chapter 6, "The Scrolls and Early Christianity: How They Are Related and What They Share," was originally published as "The Dead Sea Scrolls and Early Christianity," parts 1 and 2, in *Bible Review* 7/6, December 1991, and *Bible Review* 8/1, February 1992.

Chapter 7, "Significance of the Scrolls: A New Perspective on the Texts from the Qumran Caves," was originally published as ""Significance of the Scrolls," in *Bible Review* 6/5, October 1990.

PHOTOGRAPHY AND ART CREDITS

Artists Rights Society (ARS), New York / ADAGP, Paris © 2007: 54 (photograph by Bridgeman-Giraudon / Art Resource, NY)

Baruch Safrai: 23 (bottom left and bottom right)

Beno Rothenberg: 22, 24, 26, 28

Biblical Archaeology Society: 10

David Harris: 8 (top), 9 (bottom), 14 (bottom), 34, 40, 58, 67, 68, 76, 92 (top)

Erich Lessing / Art Resource, NY: 57

Estate of John M. Allegro: back cover (middle), 14 (top), 48 (top)

Estate of Yigael Yadin: back cover (top), 49, 88

Garo Nalbandian: 32 (left), 48 (bottom)

Giraudon / Art Resource, NY: 57

Hershel Shanks: 6, 32 (right), 36 (top), 65, 69, 71, 73 (top), 92 (bottom)

Israel Antiquities Authority: 17, 45, 46 (bottom), 47, 60, 72, 74, 84, 85, 91

Israel Musem, Jerusalem: 18, 19 (top), 37

John Trever: back cover (bottom), 8 (bottom), 11, 12, 44 (top), 51, 59, 64

Lawrence H. Schiffman: 87

Scala / Art Resource, NY: 56 (top), 77

Syndics of Cambridge University Library, Cambridge University Library T-S 10K6: 90

Werner Braun, Jerusalem: front cover (bottom), 19 (bottom), 38, 39 (left), 62

Zev Radovan (www.BibleLandPictures.com): front cover (top), title page, 9 (top), 15, 16, 20, 33 (bottom), 36 (bottom), 42, 46 (top), 56 (bottom), 66, 73 (bottom), 78, 82, 94